How to Make a Cake Rise

500 kitchen tips and tricks I wish my mother had told me

Ⓟ

This edition published by Parragon in 2012

Parragon
Queen Street House
4 Queen Street
Bath BA1 1HE, UK

ISBN: 978-1-4454-7391-8

Printed in China

Author: Manidipa Mandal
Editor: Fiona Biggs
Illustrators: Kunal Kundu, Suresh Kumar, Rajita Kashyap, Nitin Chawla
Layout: Eleven Arts
Cover design: Tracy Killick

Warning
This book is intended only for adults (aged 18 and over) and the kitchen tips and hints contained in this book should not be used by children under 18.

When using any kitchen equipment or other products in conjunction with this book, you should follow all instructions and warnings given by the manufacturers and only use such equipment and products for the purpose for which they were intended.

The publishers accept no liability for any loss or injury sustained as a result of using any of the tips and hints contained in this book.

The information in this book is for general guidance only and may not be suitable for all individuals. Please consult your health professional if in doubt.

Picture acknowledgements
The publishers would like to thank the Advertising Archives for the use of the cover images.

Contents

The Right Equipment

Choosing your gadgets and tools; getting the best use from them; maximizing efficiency and ease of use; even multitasking with common tools!

■ Pottering around

1. Pottery for the pot

Unglazed pottery, such as terracotta, can be tricky to cook in – but it can do wonderful things to food if you follow the instructions carefully.

- Avoid using it in the microwave unless it is specifically made for the purpose.
- Season before you use it for the first time by soaking in water, then filling with water with a layer of oil on top and simmering (on the hob or in the oven, as indicated by the manufacturer) until dry.

2. Spotless pots

Unglazed pottery absorbs moisture and food stains and isn't easy to wash up.

- Don't use any abrasive harsher than baking soda on unglazed pottery, or you could scratch the surface badly.
- Rinse with plenty of water to flush out any bits lodged in the tiny pores.
- Allow to air dry for a couple of days after washing – just because the surface feels dry, it doesn't mean it's dry to the core. If possible, place in a sunny position by an open window to draw out moisture.

3. Use lower temperatures for glassware

Glass retains heat longer than any other material used for baking.

- Keep an eye on your glass dishes when baking – the heat retained by the glass can cause overcooking, quicker browning and uneven cooking (those parts in contact with the container will cook faster than those raised off the surface, especially when roasting meat).
- For most baked dishes, reducing the temperature by 4–5°C/10–12°F after putting the item in the oven will reduce the chances of burning.
- Be very careful to avoid moisture coming in contact with hot glass – either from your hands or from the work surface.

4. The magic of silicone

Silicone bakeware needs no greasing – cakes pop out readily, biscuits slide off at a nudge. It is cool to touch within minutes of removal from the oven. You can even freeze batter in it and transfer straight to the oven – less washing up!

It needs some care, though:

- Foods sometimes brown unevenly.
  - Because of their flexibility, larger containers or heavily filled ones need support from a baking sheet placed underneath. This can cause the base to brown faster.
    - If crumpled or crushed repeatedly, silicone bakeware can crack.
    - Greasing leaves silicone tacky!

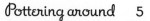

5. Keep your enamel bright

Resilient as they might seem, enamel pans can chip or scratch if roughly handled.

- Don't scrub them with bleach, steel wool or abrasive powders.
- Clean them with half a lemon dipped in borax, or buff with a paste made of bread soda and a little water.

6. A wok for all seasons

Season a traditional carbon-steel wok for years of service.

- Wash your new wok and dry on high heat.
- When smoking hot, wipe the inner surface with rapeseed oil – or another oil with a high smoking point.
- Return to heat.
- Repeat the heat-and-season cycle twice; rinse and dry.
- You now have a fairly non-stick wok that won't rust readily. It may, however, darken with use.
- After every use, wash gently – no abrasives!
- If you notice rust spots or food 'catches' more than usual, gently remove deposits with fine steel wool; re-season.

7. Smooth as steel

Stainless steel is one of the most versatile cooking materials – sturdy, with a good heat response, no rusting or tarnishing.

However, there are a couple of things you'll need to avoid for your best-quality stainless to stay that way:

- Don't wash up with steel wool! It leaves scratches.
- Rinse immediately and thoroughly after cooking acidic or salty foods. Never leave them in the pan to cool. Acids and salt pit the surface of steel!
- Dry promptly to avoid white water spots.
- Avoid overheating – it can cause rainbowing (*see Tip 8*).

8. Avoid the rainbow effect

If you notice rainbow-hued smudges on your saucepans, you're cooking on a higher heat than is good for them!

This is most obvious on stainless steel, but anodised aluminium is also susceptible. Ultimately, this will shorten the life of your utensils.

- Make sure the flame extends to only two thirds the diameter of your pans.
- Don't leave an empty pan on the stove too long – when your hand 'feels the heat' at 5 cm/ 2 inches above the surface, you should start cooking.

9. Silver and steel?

Never soak silver and stainless steel utensils together – the silver will turn black!

10. Look after the family silver!

Although versatile, silver is one of the more delicate metals.

Here's a list of things to avoid:

- Rough handling – because silver is quite soft and yields readily to pressure, you must be careful not to bend, twist or apply too much pressure.
- Abrasives – silver will scratch readily.
- Haphazard polishing – work in light strokes in only one direction, or you'll end up with a 'crazed' surface!

- Egg – this is one of the worst tarnishers.
- Rubber – rubber bands can damage silverware even through layers of tissue paper, so keep all rubber well away from those spoons!
- Moisture – place a sachet of silica gel in the silver drawer to delay tarnishing.
- Acid and bleach – wrap in acid-free paper or soft well-worn cloth.
- Steel – see Tip 9.

11. Keep your copper shining bright

Bright copper pots and pans aren't just fabulous to look at, the great conductivity means a good sturdy piece should get a lot of use. Buy pieces that are lined with stainless steel, otherwise they'll react with anything acidic: vinegar, fruit, tomatoes, even eggs!

Sadly, the gleaming surface will still tarnish on the outside, even if you keep it spotless. You can revive the mirror shine:

- Rub with half a lemon dipped in salt.
- Leave for just a minute (and no longer than two!).
- Rinse thoroughly.
- Dry with a soft cloth, wiping thoroughly.

Can you see your face in it?

12. Hard water pitfalls

Hard water and salt can leave white spots. This is not just an eyesore – on some materials it is advance notice of damage. Fine porcelain or crystal could end up with a permanent yellowish stain; metal utensils could become pitted.

- Wash by hand and dry thoroughly to avoid spots.
- Avoid adding salt to an empty pan – except to gently scour away burnt-on food (soaking with baking soda should be your first resort).
- When you season foods, allow the liquid to come to the boil first; stir until salt dissolves before removing from heat.

13. One-handed chopping

Chefs mince herbs so beautifully with just their cook's knife and the standard chopping board. That's because they've had lots of practice.

Since you've got lots of other things to do besides slicing and dicing, it's worth investing in a hachoir and mezzaluna set, preferably a one-handed model. Much faster, and no chasing the sprigs back to the knife with every few passes.

14. No-boil sterilizing

If the thought of boiling all those jars puts you off making your own jams and preserves (*see Tip 156*), heave a sigh of relief and turn on the oven!

- Preheat to 180°C/350°F/Gas Mark 4 while you put the jars through a warm rinse – either in the dishwasher or by hand.
- Instead of drying them with a tea towel place them in the oven for 10 minutes, and you're ready to fill 'em up!

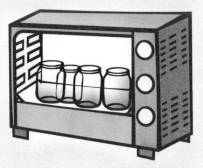

15. Flavour saver

Garlic is lovely in so many foods, from roasts to stews to dips. Peeling it can be a pain, though. Here's a time- and trouble-saver:

- Pop several heads of garlic into a sturdy freezer bag.
- Using the base of a small glass bottle or spice jar, gently crush the garlic pods to loosen the peel – no mess or sticky, smelly hands.
- Use a fork to scrape out the loose garlic skins and bung the bag in the freezer for when you need it later.

You'll never be short of flavour again. By the way, you can use a bottle or jar to lightly crush spices or soften herbs to release their aromas too, if you don't have a mortar and pestle.

16. Fine pin!

Need a clean rolling pin in the middle of a batch of furious baking?

- Remove the label from a wine bottle and use that.
- If you have only full bottles, wrap one in clingfilm and roll away!
- To clean, wash the label-free bottle – glass cleans up easily; simply unwrap the full bottle and discard the clingfilm!
- Just make sure the bottles aren't so chilled as to 'sweat', or you'll end up with soggy, sticky dough!

This is very handy when you are making different kinds of pastry or dough, both savoury and sweet, on the same day.

17. Labour-saving oven liners

If you bake a lot, you probably have to put a lot of elbow grease into cleaning the oven – sweeping out crumbs, softening spills, degreasing…

To minimize labour, start by protecting the surface – the oven 'floor' gets the worst of it.

- Reuse kitchen foil from tenting roasts or refrigerating foods to line the oven 'floor'.
- Foil bags, cut up one side and unfolded, can be used too.
- Lay foil with the food-stained or greasy side uppermost.
- When the oven has cooled, ease out carefully (to hold spills in), scrunch up and bin!

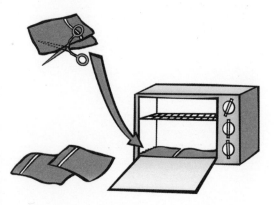

18. Slice with string

Waxed cotton thread or dental floss (unflavoured) makes light work of splitting delicate sponge cakes into layers or slicing squishy roulades.

- To cut a cake in half horizontally, use a toothpick to 'dot' a guideline along the side. Level the string along it, cross over ends and pull together.
- For roulades, use like cheese wire. Hold the thread under your thumb on one side; draw it taut by the other end and slice!
- This works for soft to medium-hard cheese too.
- It lets children slice rolls of dough until they're old enough to wield a knife.
- Good for most soft rolls or wraps – Japanese-style egg rolls, cinnamon rolls, a 'cylinder' of mousse…

19. Versatile vegetable scrub!

No, this isn't a recipe for a body scrub – it's a new use for loofahs and exfoliating mitts. Now you can use them to scrub vegetables such as potatoes and carrots, even courgettes and aubergines. They're much gentler than those scratchy nylon bristles that rip the peel and may even score the flesh of softer veggies.

Keep a separate one for use in the bath!

20. Scissors are safer (and swifter)...

When:

- Snipping tubular herbs or vegetables such as chives
- Topping and tailing beans
- Trimming leeks
- Slicing up bacon or ham strips
- Cutting fat and tendon off meats
- Butterflying prawns
- Spatchcocking chickens and other poultry

It will be quicker and easier than using a knife. It also leaves your chopping board clean.

21. Faster than a speeding microwave!

A pressure cooker makes shorter work of cooking for a crowd than a microwave oven.

- Choose the right size, or you'll waste fuel and/or food.
- Check the handle – it needs to be comfortable even when hot and full. Exposed metal bits along the underside can scald!
- A quick-release feature lowers the pressure fast. Never open a cooker until the pressure has dissipated – a steam burn is worse than boiling water!
- Instead of old-fashioned vent weights that rock and hiss, opt for calibrated spring-valve rods – quieter, safer, easier to use.

22. Creamy café

For your everyday espresso, choose a smaller pot rather than a larger one.

- The trick to a smooth, full-flavoured coffee with a nice rich crema on top is to pass the minimum quantity of water through the maximum quantity of grounds.
- You'll only get the froth from that first cupful! Which means a two-cup espresso maker is best.
- Pour an inch into both cups before you top them up.

Keep the larger pots and the 6-cup worktop machines for larger gatherings when you need to make a lot of espresso quickly.

23. Frost-free freezing

If you don't have a frost-free freezer, do a fortnightly defrost.

- Transfer all food to a thermos bag.
- Switch off the freezer.
- Line shelves with towels.
- Place another towel in the bottom of the freezer or on the floor beneath to catch spills.
- Pour hot water into shallow metal containers placed on the shelves. Shut the door. (Replace hot water as it cools, until all ice melts.)
- Wipe interior with a solution of baking soda in water; dry thoroughly.
- Turn on the freezer. Wait half an hour before replacing foods.

24. Minimize mould

A periodic vinegar wipe will keep the door seal on your freezer from sprouting mould or mildew in the creases.

25. Quick fix for a smelly fridge

When your refrigerator gets that musty odour but you haven't time to clean it out thoroughly:

- Put some coffee grounds in a shallow tin with holes poked in the lid. Place it in the fridge for a few hours to kill any nasty niffs and absorb moisture.

This is just a quick fix – you will have to use the baking soda solution eventually, and better sooner than when the mould gets a grip!

26. Blend it clean

The easiest way to clean a blender is to actually run it on empty!

- Run it half filled with hot water and a few drops of concentrated dishwashing liquid.

27. Mint-fresh mixer

All those lovely Asian spice pastes we've lately adopted are storehouses of health. But they (and even the humble carrot or juicy berries, all full of antioxidants) can stain the plastic bowl of your food processor or mixer. The flavours will also linger – so that delicate vichyssoise will smell of curry! The good news is that many of these pigments are fat-soluble, rather than water-soluble.

- Try oiling the jar or bowl before you process the colourful stuff! It should keep stains from lodging too deeply.
- What won't wash away can often be coaxed out with an oil-moistened rag or kitchen towel.
- Use a pinch of enzyme-based detergent to take out all of the residue, then rinse very thoroughly.
- To get rid of the smell, try pulsing a few mint leaves or used lemon rinds – it should refresh your processor.

28. How to hollow a pumpkin

Yes, you can buy one of those 'claws' to scoop the stringy bits out of a pumpkin. But, honestly, how many times a year will you use it?

- Your trusty pasta server, which dollops out the spaghetti on a weekly basis anyway, will do the job just as well.
- If you've got good wrist action, your ice cream scoop will work too.

29. The slice is right!

Make the most of that egg slicer or tomato slicer gadget you hardly ever use.

- Make quick work of a bowlful of potatoes boiled for a salad.
- Clean mushrooms with a stiff-bristled natural brush and pop in the slicer.
- Those cute blobs of mozzarella or petit Suisse should slice up a treat too.
- Slicing up marzipan for biscuits and cake decorations? Put it right here!
- Sausages (softer ones such as frankfurters, Cumberland or black pudding) may take a few chops to do from end to end – it's still worth it when you have a party's worth of people to feed.
- That tomato slicer will have fun with bananas, unpeeled kiwi fruit and kumquats – *so* much neater, and easier to eat.

30. Hammer and hatchet

These might sound like odd tools for the kitchen, but they are handy for splitting open large, thick-skinned vegetables – such as pumpkins – and shellfish.

The 'hammer' should be a sturdy, long-handled wooden mallet. The 'hatchet' is ideally a large, heavy-bladed cleaver – the Oriental kind with a metal handle all cast in one piece is best.

Please take care with hands and fingers!

- To crack a pumpkin open, use a controlled, careful swing to embed the cleaver lightly in the flesh (make sure the pumpkin is stable and won't roll about if rocked a little). Delivering a sharp tap or two from the mallet should swing the blade all the way in and split it in half.
- The mallet is handy for cracking up crab claws and shells after cooking. Easy does it! You don't want shell shrapnel flying everywhere.

■ Mindful maintenance

31. Tangled tongs and tines

We all have at least one kitchen drawer of awkward implements, all tangled up:

- barbecue tongs
- turkey baster
- melon baller
- tea ball
- measuring spoons
- pizza wheel

… and the kitchen fairy alone knows what else.

Sort them out:

- Mount softboard inside a cabinet door; add hooks. Hang up small objects with loops – measuring spoons, tea balls.
- For the rest, use cardboard cylinders from used-up rolls of kitchen paper and foil.
- Tape one end shut with masking tape.
- Pop tools in these 'sleeves', label along the sides and stuff scrunched-up foil or paper to 'close'.
- Arrange neatly in the drawer.

32. Oil the boards

If you scour your wooden chopping boards after every use they may split.

- Once a fortnight or so, rub your chopping board with a little salad oil to season it. (You can use some kitchen paper dipped in oil to do this.)
- Make sure the chopping board is absolutely dry, though, or you'll trap moisture – which in turn encourages nasties to take up residence, not to mention making the wood swell and warp.

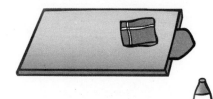

33. Carbon care

Carbon steel knives are fantastic for the way they hold their edge yet hone easily, but they do require a bit of care as they can rust (unlike the rust-resistant stainless steel).

- Wash carbon steel blades immediately after use in hot water and dry quickly.
- When completely dry, smear a drop of vegetable oil on the blade to stave off rust.
- Do not use carbon steel on vegetables that are rich in anthocyanin pigments – red cabbage, purple carrots, beetroot, aubergines, berries and blood oranges. You could end up with a distressingly blue-black dish!

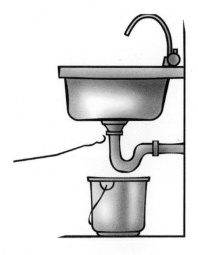

34. Blocked bend?

Kitchen sink filling up fast?

- Try bailing it out and flushing the drain with soda crystals and hot water. If it's still blocked try a proprietary drain cleaner.
- If that doesn't work, the blockage may be in the trap in the u-shaped bend under the sink. Put a bucket underneath to catch the overflow and debris, and open it up. Use the hooked end of a wire hanger to draw out what's blocking the pipe – do *not* push it further in.

35. Rubbish disposal

Some foods can actually be the death of the garbage disposal unit in your sink. It's meant for scraps, really – it's not an all-out refuse handler.

Avoiding pushing through foods that are very greasy, hard or fibrous, such as:

- Raw woody carrots
- Sugarcane stems
- Ears of corn (even if cooked!)
- Uncooked grains or pulses
- Large bones or tough cartilage
- Raw skin from fish or meat, including pork rind (even cooked)
- Oil or fat

Warning: Never put inorganic matter, such as plastic or foil, in the unit.

Kitchen Safety

Precautions for working with water, fire and electricity—all together! How to handle sharp and hot objects—with minimal risk! Emergency action and precautionary measures, too.

■ Safety start-up

36. Non-slip floors

It's all very well to add warmth to a cold hard surface, but a rug that slides on a slippery surface puts you at risk of tripping and falling.

- Restrict the use of unbacked rugs to rougher surfaces such as stone flags, wood or non-slip tiles.
- For high-shine and polished surfaces, use rugs with a rubber backing.
- Avoid rugs and mats in the kitchen; the smallest stumble with a pan of hot liquid can land you in hospital.
- In the bathroom too, avoid loose floor coverings – a mat with rubberized non-slip backing in front of the bath should be the only one here.

37. The family that's safe together...

You need to be sure that the whole family knows the safety rules – one of the best ways of doing this is to gather them together to help make a meal.

- Check their knife technique – chopping food in the wrong way with a knife that isn't sharp enough leads to many accidents in the kitchen.
- Show them how to carry vessels containing hot liquid.
- Teach them how and when to use the fire extinguisher and fire blanket (*see Tip 39*).
- If anyone has a food allergy, this is a great opportunity for learning about avoiding food contamination and planning meals for special needs.

And, of course, cooking with others also means someone else is watching your back (which may be to the oven or hot-water tap!).

38. Cook's little helpers

Children love helping in the kitchen – you can even include toddlers if you take a few precautions.

- Warn them that the stove and oven are strictly for adults only.
- Make 'lab coats' out of adult shirts with short sleeves (or cut away the sleeves).
- Show them how to measure ingredients, sift flour, mix batters, shell peas and spread toppings.
- Cutting with knives is not for the under fives. Children should start with blunt-tipped scissors – good enough for beans, ham, cheese and even toast!

39. Drop and roll

Fires happen, and they are highly likely to happen in the kitchen.

• Should your clothes or hair catch fire, don't try to run away – drop to the floor on the spot and roll over until flames are extinguished.

Teach children this lesson as soon as they can understand what fire is!

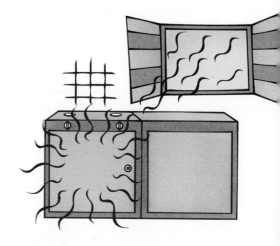

40. Smell gas? Get out!

Gas leaks can be life-threatening.

• Make sure all family members know and recognize the odour of gas.
• If you smell it, you should immediately get out of the house and go to a trusted neighbour to phone for help from there.
• On no account should you try to switch on or off any lights or fans, or try to use the phone at home – the smallest spark can provide ignition.

■ Contamination alert!

41. Separate for pets

If you have a pet, be extra careful to avoid contamination between human and animal foods.

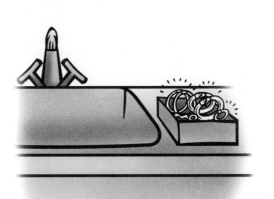

- Keep your pet's food preparation equipment away from yours; if possible, designate a separate area of the kitchen for preparing pet food.
- Have a separate can opener, spoon and fork, clearly labelled (or bearing a doggie or kitty motif), so even strangers to your home don't accidentally use them for humans.
- Wash the pet's bowls and other equipment separately, and disinfect all surfaces near the sink thoroughly before bringing your own utensils into that zone.
- When washing, make sure there are no washed 'people utensils' draining or drying near the sink that might get splashed.

42. Ditch the bling

Top chefs don't wear rings at work. Rings harbour germs that a quick lather and rinse won't get rid of.

- Clean up before you cook – take off watches, rings, bracelets and bangles. Keep a closed basket on the worktop by the door or on the kitchen table, so you remember as soon as you walk in.
- Place a small decorative ceramic box next to the sink – a bright one will remind you to put valuables there before you splash into the soapy water.

43. Safe barbecuing

A barbecue means a lot of alternating between raw and cooked meats, providing ample opportunity for contamination.

- Put a folding table to one side of the barbecue, not too close to the heat.
- Place a large tub of water on the table, with a pump dispenser bottle of disinfectant soap, and a few clean towels.
- Wash your hands after touching raw meat – each time.
- Use a fresh towel every time you dry your hands.

■ Cautious cooking

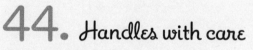

44. Handles with care

This is especially crucial with young children at home, but even an all-adult household would do well to follow this rule.

- Turn the handles of all saucepans on the hob towards the back.
- Install a protective guard around the hob, to prevent inquisitive little fingers reaching up to take hold of a handle.
- Never keep more than one knife on the chopping board or worktop at a time.
- Rest knives parallel to the front of, not perpendicular to, the worktop so that if you lean on a knife inadvertently it won't shoot outwards.

45. With knobs on!

Children love pressing switches, especially on gadgets that will 'go' – such as washing machines or microwave ovens with turntables.

- If you have small children at home, get safety covers for appliance knobs.
- Even older children should use the microwave oven only under supervision.
- If you can, install a built-in 'appliance garage' unit with a rolling shutter you can lock. If you put a socket strip along the back wall, you can plug in many smaller appliances in situ – waffle iron, toaster, coffee maker, microwave – and have nothing to 'put away' when you've finished.

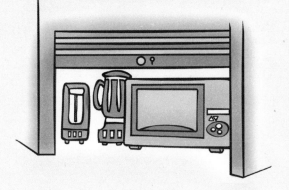

46. Oil spill alert!

Grease on the floor is a sure recipe for disaster, or at least a painful tumble.

- Throw flour over the grease to absorb it quickly, pressing down and moving the flour around as needed to absorb the grease.
- Now you should be able to brush most of the mess into your dustpan.
- Soap and water should take care of the rest.

47. If there's smoke, there's fire

As in all the other rooms in the house – indeed, even more so – you need a smoke detector in the kitchen. However, this is also the one room that already has an open flame and it could readily get smoky!

Look for a smoke detector alarm with a silencer feature that allows you to hush it up while you chargrill peppers!

48. Fabric and fire don't mix

You can't do without your tea towels and oven gloves, but most fabric is flammable and you're likely to be working with an open flame.

- Avoid having fabric curtains along the same wall as an oven or hob.
- Don't wear long sleeves or loose garments while cooking. Roll up your sleeves and put on an apron, preferably one made of a fire retardant material.
- Never hang tea towels or oven gloves from the handle of an oven that is in use, or behind or above the hob (from a rod along the back of the worktop or from hooks attached to the chimney hood, for instance).

49. Safe plastic and paper

Paper is another highly flammable material, and plastics can exhibit a range of unpleasant reactions to heat.

- Do not keep kitchen paper anywhere near cooking appliances.
- Avoid storing either food or utensils and appliances in paper packaging, even within cabinets. (The fridge is safer, though, being cold.)
- If in doubt about a plastic's capacity to withstand heat, keep the utensil clear of the oven and hob and certainly don't use it when microwaving!
- Avoid using plastic or plastic-lined aprons or gloves – if they melt or catch fire, they will stick painfully to your flesh.

50. Stand back!

Be conscious of how you carry yourself near open flames and cooking appliances.

- Tie back your hair securely while preparing food – it's not only hygienic, but a safety prerequisite.
- Avoid cooking with artificial nails on – not only could they catch painfully while you handle dough or grate a carrot, proximity to heat can cause them to burn or melt while still on your fingers!
- Never allow yourself (or a family member) to fall into the habit of leaning against the kitchen units or worktop as you cook. You might absent-mindedly lean too close to the hot hob or press a knee against the hot oven door.
- Explain to children that touching the oven door is taboo; only the door handle may be touched and that only with gloves on.
- That's a good reason to have the oven at eye level, out of reach of children.

51. You can't stand the heat

Burns are an ever-present risk in the kitchen, so learn to respect heat.

- Never place a hot pot, cup or even a spoon near the edge of the counter. This is especially crucial if you have children or pets. A dog jumping up to grab a dangling spoon could end up with a badly burnt tongue; and even you might accidentally knock the coffeepot over.
- Hanging rods along the backsplash maximizes your storage space. But never hang things directly behind the stove where you might have to reach across bubbling liquids or flickering flames for a ladle.
- If your hob has front and back burners, use the back burners as much as possible. It means a child won't be able to grab a saucepan nor a pet reach into the flame under it – and you won't inadvertently brush against hot utensils (*see Tip 44*).

52. Food on fire!

Keep a fire extinguisher and fire blanket in the kitchen. Some additional tips:

- If food in a pan catches fire, turn off the hob and place a lid on the pan (to cut off air). Let it cool (about half an hour) before moving.
- If fat catches fire, smother with baking soda – it also helps scour off burnt-on food and grease. Never pour water on hot fat!
- If the fire's in the oven, pull the plug and keep the door closed.
- If the barbecue catches fire, close the lid (or use a large metal bowl). Otherwise scoop some soil over it.

53. Oil safety

Pan drippings make a delicious gravy, but because they have a high fat content, you must take care.

- Never place a pan of drippings or an oil bottle near a naked flame – it could easily be set alight.
- Make it a habit to reach for the oil, pour and replace it in one single, fluid movement.

54. Yellow for danger

If your gas hob is burning with yellowish rather than blue flames, this shows it isn't functioning optimally. Not only is this inefficient use of the gas fuel, it could signal a potentially dangerous problem.

- Get the hob checked and serviced as soon as you notice the problem.

- Always turn on the gas before you put a pot on the hob. That way it flares up faster and upwards, and you aren't 'working blind' (very risky!).

■ Wise up around watts

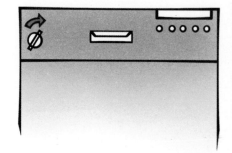

55. Microwave with caution

- Cook in covered containers to avoid splatters. But uncover carefully – a sudden gush of steam or splash of boiling liquid can cause painful burns. Always open the lid away from your face, easing up the side opposite you first.
- When using clingfilm to cover food, poke vents in it to let steam escape.
- Prick dense foods or those with 'skins' – egg yolks, sausages, cakes of tinned fish or spam, potatoes, tomatoes – to prevent 'explosions'!
- Many unmarked ceramics are microwave-safe. However, if a dish has any metallic trim, do not use it!

56. Fight the flicker

Flickering oven lights, a sluggish blender or a fluorescent strip that dims when you turn on the dishwasher might all indicate overloaded sockets or faulty wiring.

- Get the electrician in and fix it pronto – nowhere is this more crucial than the gadget-heavy kitchen area.

57. Keep the watts from water

Another kitchen duo that doesn't mix – electricity and water.

- Never operate an electrical appliance near the sink. If it falls in, even while switched off, it could electrocute someone.
- If you ever do drop a plugged-in appliance into water, immediately dry your hands and switch off the power at the mains, then unplug the appliance from the socket before attempting to lift it out.
- Use power sockets equipped with a circuit interrupter that senses any leakage of electricity – from a fault or from immersion of an appliance in water – and switches it right off.

■ Serving safeguards

58. Clear exit

When leaving the kitchen balancing hot food in breakable containers, you can minimize the risk of accidents:

- Avoid carrying a tray or container so large you can't see where you are putting your feet.
- Don't have swing doors at the kitchen entrance – it obstructs your view both as you enter and leave, making collisions more likely.
- Install a bright light just inside the doorway if your kitchen opens into a corridor, so that anyone leaving will cast a sharp shadow visible to someone coming up the corridor.
- Avoid having a threshold across the door or a difference of levels that may cause you to trip or lose your footing.

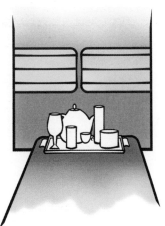

59. Don't freeze those leftovers!

It may seem tempting, but leftovers contaminated with saliva are a health hazard.

- It is especially important not to store the 'leftovers' from a baby's bowl of food.
- You might just get away with refrigerating the remains of your own meal if you will be the one eating it, but even this is risky.
- On no account should you mix food left over from what you set out on the table and what you put away before serving.

60. Don't mix medication and meals

You always seem to have more medication in the house when you have young children.

- Keep a special set of spoons and measures for medicinal substances. That way, no one will inadvertently drink cough syrup from a shot glass!

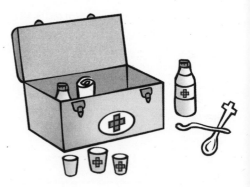

Shopping and Storage

All about food selection and storage. Fruit and veg, dairy products, meat and poultry, fish and seafood — how to select for superior taste and nutrition, and how to keep them at their best in your fridge or larder.

■ Clever shopping

61. You can keep your phone on

Keep your mobile phone handy in the supermarket.

- Use the calculator function to compare unit prices of various brands and sizes instead of guessing or revisiting your mental maths skills. This is not the time!

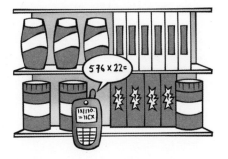

62. Check those expiry dates

Before you decide to bulk-buy that special offer, make sure you'll be able to use it all before the expiry date. Otherwise, it's no bargain!

- Always check the back of the shelf — usually packages from older lots are placed up front and newer stock is stacked at the back. This should have a later expiry date.

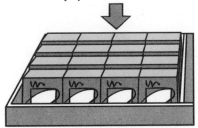

63. Frozen on the final lap

Frozen foods are meant to stay that way – *frozen!* – until you're ready to use or eat them.

- In the store, pick them up on your way out – going to the freezer last thing before paying at the till minimizes the time food spends outside the freezer.

64. Pack clever

As with shopping, so with packing (and unpacking) – there is safety in order. And nowhere more so than with frozen foods.

- Pack all the frozen foods together, so that they insulate each other against heat.
- Bring along an insulated cooler bag or box (the kind you take on picnics) to pop the frozen foods in for the journey home.
- Never pack hot food (such as warm bread fresh from the oven or a spit-roasted chicken) together with frozen.
- Never stop to shop for other things or run further errands after you've picked up frozen groceries.
- Put away the frozen food first!

65. Partner the perishables

As with the frozen food, you need to get perishables into storage quickly, so it helps if they aren't scattered across several boxes or bags, mixed up with everything else.

- Buy the inert and preserved items first — foil, kitchen paper, detergents and canned and bottled foods.
- Buy fruit, vegetables and fresh dairy products, meat, fish and bakery items on the second-last lap.
- Pack the perishables together.
- Keep raw meat away from fruit and vegetables.
- Keep dairy and cooked items separate from raw foods.

66. Look behind the labels

What goes on front is often a marketing gimmick. The real story's on ingredients lists.

- Marked 'low-fat'? Compare the 'original' — similar calories means extra sugar (to compensate for fat)!
- Your daily fat allowance is 70 g/2½ oz. If a 'diet' snack has 30 g/1 oz, where does that leave the rest of your meals?
- Does it list 'sodium'? Multiply by 2.5 for 'salt' content!
- Manmade trans fats are worse than natural ones in animal products. If it contains 'hydrogenated' or 'modified' vegetable oil, avoid it!
- Don't accept saturated instead of trans! If it reads 'trans fat-free', look out for 'palm'.

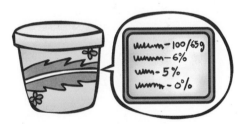

67. Take a pound of impulse

With all the marketing ploys and advertising spots, it's harder for shoppers to avoid impulse buys – indeed, the supermarket is designed to take advantage of human helplessness in the face of temptation.

• Make a list, and do your best to stick to it.
• Always put the impulse buys in a separate handheld basket, not the big shopping cart. That way, the weight will slow you (or your child) down enough to rethink your choices.
• Carry a small amount of ready cash for impulse buys and treats – a pound per person is plenty. Never pay for those with your credit card.

68. Leave the cranky child at home

Avoid taking children to the supermarket when they are not well rested and calm.

• A cranky, sleepy child is high on impulse, low on patience. You will either end up with a curtailed trip, or buy without sufficient thought – which in turn can mean poor nutritional choices and impulse purchases made to stall that tantrum.

69. Don't shop on empty

It may be best to exhaust your supplies before you replenish them. However, there are a couple of ground rules:

• Never shop on an empty stomach. You'll buy things that you really don't need.
• Never do the food shopping with a famished child in tow – that's asking for trouble.

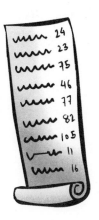

71. Clear out the clear stuff

It's tempting to use clear plastic and glass storage jars – so easy to see what's where. However, heat and light aren't best friends with most foodstuffs – and there tends to be a good mix of each in the average kitchen!

- To protect your edibles, choose metal or well-fired ceramic instead.
- Add a visual label – snap a photo of contents and tie on like a gift tag.
- Scribble the 'best before' date under it.

Now you know what's where and how fast you must use it up.

70. Bill foolish?

Always double-check the bill before paying at the till – no matter how long the list.

- You are within your rights to wait to check the receipt – don't let the queue behind dissuade you.
- Remember: computerized is not the same as error-free. Wrong barcodes get entered, specials get left out – cashiers are human after all. However, you shouldn't have to pay for human error.
- If in doubt, ask the cashier to come with you to the aisle and check up – it is not an unreasonable request, and saves time haranguing over what either of you 'thinks' is the case.

■ Fruit and veg

72. Ripe for the picking?

- Pineapples are ripe when a tugged leaf comes off readily.
- Buy bananas and papayas slightly underripe, firm and greenish. Ripen in a paper bag at room temperature.
- Mushrooms are at their prime for a day, then deteriorate rapidly.
- Go by smell, not softness, for stone fruits. They often have short seasons, so buy some ripe to eat and get enough extras to ripen gradually in a paper bag at room temperature.
- Melons and kiwi are ripe when fragrant.
- Pick fresh figs ripe for the table – they spoil soon after.

73. Too green? Or overripe?

Not all fruit ripens readily on the tree and goes on until rot sets in!

- Pineapples stop ripening once picked. Very handy!
- Some varieties of avocado don't ripen *until* picked, so don't avoid it just because it's hard – it just means it's fresh!
- Tomatoes won't ripen further in the refrigerator – so if you have too many ripe ones, putting them in the salad box may stem the rot.
- Ripe bananas blacken in the refrigerator or freezer, but the flesh is still good to eat – use them for baking or blending.
- Berries will rot rather than ripen after picking. They go mouldy and messy easily – buy them ripe, and store on a layer of kitchen paper in the fridge.

74. Brown but sweet!

Unlike blotches and bruises from poor handling, a matt browning on tree fruits is usually caused by friction with leaves.

- Browning is common on fruits near the tips of branches – and these could actually taste better because they will have had more exposure to the sun!

75. Banana tree

Bananas hasten the ripening – and spoilage – of other fruits if kept together in the fruit basket.

- You could pile them in a separate fruit bowl; but again, if they are stacked more than one deep, they'll rot quickly as the gas rises up between layers.
- A banana tree will allow air to circulate and will keep the fruit fresh for longer.

76. Citrus bright?

Don't go by colour when buying citrus fruit.

- Citrus varieties vary widely in terms of colour.
- Ripeness doesn't necessarily result in bright yellow or orange fruit! Green patches or paler hues of yellow-orange are characteristic of some varieties.
- Look instead for smooth, shiny peel – even unwaxed organic fruit won't be matt unless it's past its prime.
- Very brown fruit should be avoided. A few shallow 'scars' are fine though (*see Tip 74*).
- The fruit should have a thin skin (taking the variety into account – limes are usually thinner-skinned than lemons, so compare individual fruit of the same variety). Thicker-skinned fruit can be less juicy.
- The fruit should feel firm and heavy for its size. Avoid dents and gouges. However, loose-skinned fruit such as tangerines will be less dense than grapefruit.

78. Greens are good

It's good practice to buy root vegetables with the greens still attached.

- Beetroot, carrot, turnip and radish greens are all extremely nutritious (not just iron, they have calcium and carotene too) and tasty.
- Fresh greens prove the roots are freshly harvested and in their prime.
- When storing, wrench the greens off and store them separately from the tubers – otherwise the tops will draw moisture out of the roots and turn them woody.

77. Time for tomatoes

Tomatoes crop up in recipes all year, but are at their best in summer.

- During a glut, bottle your own concentrated purée (sealed with a layer of oil) and passata; or oven-dry.
- Off-season plum tomatoes are meatier than beef tomatoes and Hollands.
- Cherry and pear tomatoes are always sweet.
- Usually, yellow tomatoes are sweeter than red!
- In winter, canned – especially peeled whole – tomatoes in juice, no added salt, is a better buy (and cheaper) than hothouse or tropical produce.
- Purée is better than sauce for pizza or crostini toppings, when ripe (uncooked) tomatoes are scarce.

79. Beetroot greens? Stop if red!

Mostly you can tell if your greens are fresh – likewise any root vegetable attached to it – by checking for wilting, yellowing or pale spots. Those are the plants that are too old to be nutritious. Signs to look out for:

- Beetroot greens go red at the tips as they mature!
- With thick-stemmed greens such as kale, thickened veins and woody stems indicate age.
- Ageing chard and spinach are also identified by coarse stems – they aren't bad to eat if you stew them, add cream and pass through a strainer.

80. On the shelf

It's not ideal to keep salad leaves for more than a day. But if you must:

- Cleaning out the muck and discarding inedible bits can prolong refrigerator-life – as long as you dry well after washing!
- After putting them through the salad spinner, tie up loosely in a clean tea cloth before popping in the crisper drawer.
- Poke holes in a plastic bag, line with kitchen paper and put the leaves in, leaving them plenty of breathing space.
- Use within 3–4 days.

81. Play snap!

When buying okra or celery, make sure it isn't old and fibrous, or limp from long or improper storage.

- Celery stalks should break crisply and sharply.
- Discreetly snap the tips of okra – if they break crisply and fall right off, that's a pod you want. If it bends rather than breaking, leave it.
- Hold asparagus stalks at either end and snap to break – the point of breakage is always the point at which you should trim the stem, separating woody growth from tender tip. Then pare away the tough peel before cooking.

82. Edible flowers

Edible blossoms make a pretty addition to green salads as well as a great garnish for various other dishes. Grow your own – or contact a reputable nursery or farmer who will find you pesticide-free flowers for the dining table.

Good, easily available choices:
- Rocket blooms
- Borage
- Nasturtiums
- Pansies
- Blossoms of all edible herbs – from chicory to fenugreek to tarragon
- Marigolds
- Honeysuckle
- Day lilies – very good frittered!
- Roses, violets and lavender, of course.

83. Listen to your artichokes

Yes, that's right – it's fresh if it talks to you!

- To choose tender young artichokes, hold them up to your ear and squeeze.
- If they have nice moist flesh, the leaves will squeak together.
- A hollow whisper means it's drying out.

84. Little green sputnik!

It's common for the kohlrabi to be likened to an alien!

- A relation of the common cabbage, kohlrabi is milder tasting, slightly nuttier and sweetish when young, and can even be eaten raw.
- It's also surprisingly resilient to pest attacks and so it's easy to grow without pesticides.
- Choose bulbs that are less than 7.5 cm/3 inches in diameter. The bigger heads may have woody bits that need trimming.
- Diced, they make a lovely addition to stews.
- Cook any young and unblemished leaves along with the bulb – this intensifies the flavour.

85. Sweet summer's marrow

The warm-weather squashes, such as courgette and pattypans, should be harvested while still quite young, so that the rinds are edible and seeds immature.

- Look for smooth, unblemished skins – avoid any black or dark spots, as well as any browning near the tips.
- While not hard like winter marrow, summer squash too should be firm. Yet the rind should be easy to pierce (if it's too tough it's too old to eat).
- As with oranges, squash should feel heavy for its size – this means tender, dense flesh that hasn't turned fibrous or lost moisture.
- Ideally, courgette and yellow summer squashes (such as crooknecks) should be picked no more than 15 cm/6 inches long. The fingerling sizes are best to eat.
- Pattypans should be no more than 10 cm/4 inches across.
- Refrigerated in a perforated polythene bag, tender squashes will keep for 3–4 days. Any longer and you risk spoilage.

86. The whole squash

Winter marrows include pumpkins, butternut, acorn and spaghetti squash.

- Winter squashes should have hard rinds – knock on them to check.
- Cracks indicate poor handling or storage, so the flesh may not be sound.
- Green-skinned squashes may have lighter flecks, faint stripes or orange patches. But avoid pale patches and brown spots.
- Butternut squash should be a glossy tan, like an egg.
- Pumpkins should be bright orange.
- You needn't refrigerate winter marrows. Stored whole in a cool, dry place where air circulates (turn often or hang in a net bag), they'll last up to two months!

87. Pickle-free pumpkin preserving

Pumpkin is a hardy vegetable if kept dry – lucky for you, given the sizes they can grow to.

- However, once cut, they last better if left in a cool spot – minus their seeds! Which means scooping them out (*see Tip 28*).
- When you take the 'lid' off, slant your knife tip inwards so that the lid will sit snugly but not fall in later.
- Discard the stringy bits (you can save some seeds to toast with salt or sugar). If you need to store it for more than a few days, apply a light coat of petroleum jelly to the cut edges and rub some into the skin to prevent loss of moisture!
- Wipe clean before cooking – just to help flavours penetrate.

88. Basket by basket

Onions, garlic and potatoes are the most common veggies to be left out of the refrigerator. However, they do like a well-ventilated basket and keep best when separated from each other.

- A stacked bamboo steamer is perfect for the job and neat enough to sit on the most streamlined worktop.

90. Soggy in the salad box?

Yes, fresh vegetables and fruit need to retain a certain amount of moisture if they are to stay fresh. However, every time you open and close the fridge door, precipitation and condensation can add more moisture than is strictly healthy. And certain vegetables, such as salad leaves, often turn limp quickly.

- Place a layer of kitchen paper at the bottom of the salad box before you unpack the groceries.
- Wherever possible, discard polythene bags and plastic wrappings.
- Wrap individual vegetables or fruit in more kitchen paper, particularly if there are leafy greens in there.
- Do *not* store mushrooms in the salad box!
- Avoid throwing soft-stemmed herbs there too – they are better off in a jar of water in the fridge door (*see Tip 113*).

89. Cool new potatoes

Most potatoes keep better in a dark place outside the refrigerator. Strangely, it's not true of the bite-sized cuties!

- As befits their youth, baby new potatoes like to stay 'chilled'! Otherwise the warming, humid air of returning summer tends to make them go soft and ooze.
- Put them in the refrigerator – but no plastic, please, and keep the humidity low.
- A sheet of kitchen paper will soak up any excess moisture from other vegetables as well as keep them in the dark when you open the fridge door.

■ Grains and legumes

91. The hard and soft of flour

When it comes to baking cakes and bread, not all flour is milled equal.

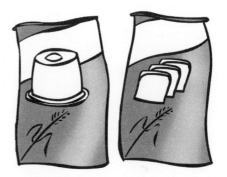

- For a truly light-as-air texture – especially for fat-free sponge and angel food cakes – it's worth seeking out cake flour or a plain flour labelled 'soft' or 'fine' instead of regular 'self-raising'. (You can always add in baking powder separately – *see Tip 237*).

92. Pasta puzzle

Should you buy fresh and turn up your nose at dried boxes of farfalle? Should you penny-pinch over plain Jane everyday pasta instead of the fancy shapes? The answer really depends on what you intend to do with it:

- In a creamy or buttery sauce, softer fresh pasta lends silkiness.
- Oil-based sauces gain heft from the dried semolina.
- Seafood and meat sauces, and even chunkier vegetable sauces, are best off with dried pasta, ideally in a shape with ridges or hollows to 'grab' the sauce.

93. Corny but sweet!

Fresh sweetcorn is a delicacy to treat with respect. The sugar in each ear of corn starts to change into insoluble starch as soon as it is picked off the plant.

- Which means you should store them for no more than a day – if you can't eat at once, it's a good idea to boil, butter (or oil) and refrigerate for a couple of days more.
- When buying, check for freshness by examining the husk first – you want tight, green wrappers and soft silk.
- Now check both ends – look for a moist yellow (not pale or browning) stem at the stalk end, firm plump kernels at the top.

94. Get gritty with grains

Pasta, rice, oatmeal, polenta… Add to the New Age granary bin:

- Amaranth: Super-nutritious; nutty with a mild pepperiness – no seasoning needed. It turns creamy when cooked in liquid; pops lightheartedly over dry heat.
- Millets: Rich in iron. Substitute for rice, wheat, barley or oats. A steamed pilaf is especially nice.
- Quinoa: High in protein, with more calcium than milk! It cooks creamy, making quinoa porridge a great breakfast for the lactose-intolerant.
- Wild rice: Doesn't keep well; expensive too. Use sparingly to perk up humbler grains (such as plain brown basmati rice).

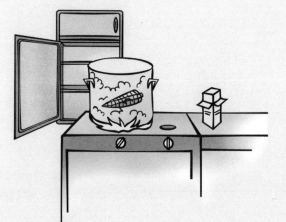

95. Long live legumes

Legumes are less prone to rancidity than grains, so they're well worth buying in bulk.

- Dried lentils and beans, in fact, keep well for up to 2–3 years – much longer than many canned foods.
- The older ones will just need longer cooking, so an overnight soak followed by pressure cooking or a spell in your slow cooker should soften them up nicely.

96. The cost of a can

How much do you actually get from a can of beans after draining and rinsing?

- Well, the typical 400 g/14 oz can should yield about 240 g/8 ½ oz of beans such as chickpeas or kidney beans. With some lighter pulses, such as lentils, you might get a little less.

■ Dairy and eggs

97. In defence of dairy

Always keep dairy products and eggs airtight against foods with strong aromas, as they absorb odours easily.

- Make sure yogurt, cream and milk are in tight-lidded containers; if not, wrap the top closely with foil or decant (but *see Tip 301*).
- Eggs should be fine in their carton; if you've thrown away the carton, you'd better pop them in a lidded plastic tub. Keep them on the top shelf of the fridge, not in the door.
- Cheese actually likes to breathe, so keep it away from the aromatic stuff; if you can't, putting it in a cardboard box is a compromise that will work as long as you use it up quickly.

98. Farm fresh eggs?

Yes, we've all heard about floating eggs in water to check their freshness. But we doubt the supermarket's offering you a bowl of water to play with.

- Inspect the shell instead – if it looks chalky, even a little bumpy like fresh plaster, that's a good indication of recent laying.
- A waxy smooth shell, attractive as it might seem, is likely to have been hanging around for too long.

99. Fresh in the whey

Buying fresh white cheese, such as mozzarella or cottage cheese?

- The kind packed in whey keeps fresh longest.
- Don't throw away the whey – it's great for kneading bread dough with. It makes for really soft, tasty, extra nutritious (whey has protein) bread.
- Just be aware that whey will stain (actually, bleach) fabric readily, so get the apron on while cooking. And double-wrap for transporting and storage.

■ Meat and poultry

100. Choosing chicken

If you're making curry or stew rather than a fancy grilled dish, don't bother getting prepared chicken breasts or thighs.

- Just ask for a fresh, whole chicken to be jointed for you, and ask for the giblets to be bagged for your stock pot.
- Don't forget to pick up a few hefty carrots and a couple of celery or leek stalks on the way out. Throw them into the pot to boil with the giblets and a bag of bouquet garni while you cook dinner.
- By the time you've eaten, the stock should be ready to strain.
- Freeze the stock and bag it for soup. There, two dishes for the price of one!

101. Lean loins

An easy guide to shopping for low-fat and lean(er) meats:

- The more marbling, the more tender and fattier. Choose less visible fat and factor in extra marinating or braising time instead.
- Look for 'round' and 'loin', as well as 'leg' cuts.

102. Humbler ham

If you can't get a whole gammon for the Sunday roast, don't despair.

- Ask for a rolled loin of pork instead – it's just as delicious, and not as salty.
- It's easy to turn into a posh roast, too – unroll and stuff with a handful of fresh herbs (pork especially likes sage), or a traditional onion stuffing, or even a few chopped prunes. Roll up and secure again.
- Either lay strips of bacon on top to keep it moist, or have some apple sauce handy for basting.

103. Superior steaks

If a great grilled dinner begins with a perfect juicy steak or plump chicken breast, the second step is the marinade.

A good trick is to marinate the meat before you freeze it:

- Put each steak into a freezer-proof polythene bag along with a portion of marinade.
- It will marinate until it freezes, and then once again while you thaw each steak in the refrigerator before cooking.
- Then all you need do is heat the frying pan, pull open the bag and slide it all in…Dinner in 10 minutes!

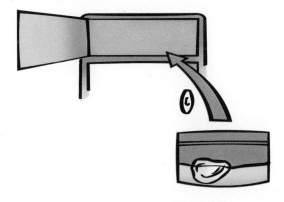

104. Frozen for choice

We're all for convenience; but not at the cost of, well, cost!

Why buy expensive ragù-style meat sauces for pasta when all you want is a meaty sauce for spaghetti?

- Keep some frozen meatballs or fresh coarse sausages in the freezer.
- To serve, thaw till you can mash them or crumble from frozen.
- Heat up with canned tomatoes, some herbs and a couple of chopped onions, and pour over pasta.

105. The value of veal

Because it comes from young calves, veal is leaner than hefty cuts from full-grown beef cattle.

- Typically it has a third less fat, which means it cooks more delicately – cooking techniques and times should be closer to poultry.
- Milk-fed veal is the premium quality – it should be pale pink with hardly any marbling, and with fine sinews.
- The darker veal from grass- or grain-fed calves is cheaper, and not as fine – but it'll still be quite delicate as long as the calf was no more than three months old. Check with your butcher.

106. Fresh bird or frozen?

While it's safe to thaw small joints of frozen poultry in the microwave, whole birds should always be thawed slowly in a fridge or at room temperature. Allow plenty of time for a frozen turkey:

- In a fridge at 4°C/39°F, allow about 10-12 hours per kilo.
- In a cool room (below 17.5°C/64°F), allow about 3-4 hours per kilo.
- At room temperature (about 20°C/68°F) allow about 2 hours per kilo.
- Take care not to allow the thawing liquid to drip onto other foods and always wash your hands thoroughly before and after handling raw meat.

107. Cold chicken?

Do you need to shove the fresh spring chicken into the freezer straight away? No, not if you mean to cook it soon.

- It's fine to let poultry sit in the fridge for up to 2 days. Just make sure it is securely wrapped and covered so that it can't drip a drop on anything else (be very afraid of salmonella!)
- Any longer, and you really ought to freeze it – for up to 6 months.
- If you like, marinate and then freeze (*see Tip 103*).

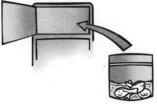

■ Seafood

108. Firm fish, please

Do the triple-test when buying fish – smell, see and touch.

- Fresh fish smells like a fresh sea breeze – briny and not 'fishy'.
- If your environment disguises smells, look closely at the eyes and scales. Loose scales, bare patches and messy fins show signs of too much age. Similarly, gills should be bright red and the eyes should be clear, not milky.
- Finally, feel the fillet. It should be firm, moist, shiny and plump – not soft, saggy or spongy.

109. When frozen is best

If the fresh looks iffy, let alone whiffy, you'd be better off fishing around in the freezer chest.

- Look for 'flash-frozen' – this means that it went from sea to freezer right away, with no time to spoil.

110. The big freeze?

How long fish will 'keep' depends on how fat it is – literally!

- Lean fish, oddly enough, keeps better than oily fish! Oily fish will keep, frozen, for just about 3 months; less oily cousins can hang about twice as long.
- Whole fish, unsurprisingly, last better than cuts.
- Don't store any fish in the refrigerator for more than a day.
- Whatever the type, wash it (even if it has been 'cleaned') when you get home, pat dry thoroughly and wrap in greaseproof paper before bagging.

111. Shell open, shell closed?

For mussels and oysters, it's not just whether they are open or closed that indicates freshness. The question is: when are they open and when are they closed?

- When buying fresh mussels, give the shells a tap – if they promptly clam up, that means they are alive, and good to eat.
- Trawl through the pot again after cooking, though. Any that still stay shut should be tossed away!

112. Spice labels

Putting spices in identical jars is neat; but if you keep them on a shelf, you won't see beyond the first row to what's at the back. They all look the same until you move the first row out of the way.

- Keep your spice jars in a shallow drawer, rather than that favourite place, a shelf over the hob.
- Tape labels across the lids instead of on the jars.
- They'll keep better too, since heat rising from the hob won't affect them.

113. Water for long herbs

Got a big bunch of fresh herbs and can't use them up at once?

- If they've got their roots or are long in the stem, soft herbs such as basil, coriander and dill can be kept on a cool worktop or in the fridge for several days – as long as they are well watered.
- Immerse the roots or stems (picked clean of lower leaves) in two fingers of water in a tall glass or jar.
- Place a plastic bag over the top and secure at the rim to minimize moisture loss.

114. Wraps for short herbs

For fresh herbs with short stems, or just leaves (such as sage), the watering approach won't work. Yet, left to themselves in the fridge, they will wilt within hours. Wrap them up to prevent loss of moisture.

- Dampen a clean piece of muslin or a tea towel with cold water.
- Place a few leaves or sprigs at one end and roll up loosely.
- Refrigerate and use within 2–3 days.

115. Dry your own

You can dry your own fresh herbs, as long as you buy them with the stems.

- Bunch herbs together by the stems into loose posies.
- Pop the 'heads' inside a perforated paper bag to protect from light and dust and tie them together by the stems, leaving a loop to hang by.
- Hang in an airy place away from direct sunlight for 2–3 weeks to dry.
- Store whole posies in a canister or slip them inside polythene bags and tie at the base.

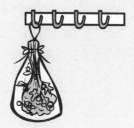

116. Toasted and hammered

Many spices such as cumin, coriander, chilli and cardamom – as well as dried woody herbs – release maximum flavour when dry-roasted whole and ground in a mortar and pestle.

• Grind only when ready to use.

117. Best not dried

It's on the shelf, but it's possibly best avoided:

• Dried basil
• Dried chives
• Dried dill
• Dried fenugreek
• Dried parsley

118. As good or better dry

Some herbs are actually better dry, or as good and cheaper than fresh:

• Oregano
• Thyme
• Mint (but don't keep for too long).

119. Hot green corns

White pepper is known to be milder than black. And fresh green peppercorns are gentler than either.

- Use them in the mix of ingredients for steak au poivre.
- Partner them with more delicate foods such as really fresh fish.

120. Chilli gone cold?

Chilli sauce and condiments flavoured with the spice keep better than the powdered pepper!

- Chilli powder doesn't lose potency but goes musty and risks spoilage.
- Don't buy more than a couple of months' supply at a time.
- Store tightly closed in a cool, dry place – but not the fridge either!

121. Horseradish hot

Unlike many spicy condiments – such as mustard, salsa and harissa – horseradish paste and sauce lose potency pretty fast.

- Use within a few months.

- Whole dried chillies, though, are happy to stand in the sun.
- Growing your own? Chilli loves sunlight – so move it out of the shade and leave well alone in dull grey weather.

122. The big daddy of cardamom

The cardamom pods you typically buy are pale green in colour. However, it is worth seeking out the larger (about twice the size), dried black cardamom pods for some dishes.

- Any dish with a slightly sweet base benefits from the stronger zest of this spice.
- Use only the seeds, crushed, discarding the pod itself – it's too astringent.
- Try it in coconut-based curries, pumpkin stew, roasted parsnips and carrots, rice pudding and chocolate desserts.
- It also makes a lovely palate cleanser to chew on after a meal. Offer a single pod, pressed open to expose the seeds, with an after-dinner cuppa.

123. Chilled seeds and nuts

Both sesame seeds and oil are frequently used in Eastern cooking.

- However, sesame goes off quickly. It's best to store it in the refrigerator.
- Do the same with peanuts and tree nuts that haven't been roasted or toasted.

124. Vinegar – plain and simple?

Unlike several other condiments and oils, vinegar is not a particularly expensive ingredient on its own. If you're paying a premium, check that you aren't buying 'packaging'!

- Does the vinegar contain expensive inclusions? Exotic fruit, for instance, but not common herbs.
- Does it derive from an uncommon source that is very seasonal, for example raspberries?
- Is it aged? This applies only to balsamic vinegar, which can be casked in oak, cherry, ash, chestnut and whatnot. And yes, this is the one that pares a pretty penny off your purse.
- Can't find just the vinegar your recipe requires? A little citrus or grape juice (for wine vinegars) or apple juice (for cider) will do the trick in most dishes.

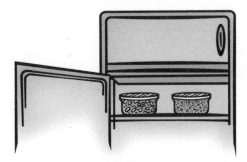

125. Laudable libations

You don't have to break out the Dom Perignon for cooking with. But whatever liquor you use in a dish is there for its flavour (which intensifies as the alcohol evaporates), so do choose a decent bottle.

• If you wouldn't drink it, don't cook with it!

126. Sweet stuff!

• Brown sugar brings extra moisture to your cake! (Which also means clumping – crusts of stale bread and paper towels in the jar help delay the inevitable.)
• Molasses? More moisture still. Expect chewy rather than fluffy results.
• Caster sugar's the stuff for fluff – soufflés, sauces, sponges.
• Icing 'sugar' contains starch, so isn't as sweet! But it dissolves quickly – sprinkle at the last moment for sparkle.
• The darker the sugar, the more complex the flavour. Plain white is best for delicate foods – the bouquet of Darjeeling tea is quite drowned by robust brown beet sugar!

■ Local, seasonal, organic – in order

127. Seasonal specials

Much of our supermarket produce these days is available all year round, irrespective of climate and time of year.

However, some things are still best local and seasonal – not just for the environment, but in terms of flavour too.

128. In spring, savour

- artichokes
- asparagus
- peas
- spring onions
- spring greens and salads

129. Summer specialities

- beans – broad and runner
- corn
- cucumbers
- okra
- summer squash (such as courgettes)
- tomatoes
- sweet peppers
- melons
- fresh figs
- mangoes
- pawpaws
- stone fruit – apricots, peaches, plums and nectarines
- berries – strawberries early on, then blueberries, raspberries and blackberries
- cherries
- rhubarb

130. Autumn glories

- Brussels sprouts
- kohlrabi
- leeks
- parsnips
- sweet potatoes
- swedes and turnips
- winter squash (butternut and acorn)
- apples
- cranberries
- pears
- grapes
- pomegranates
- fennel

131. Wait for winter for

- oranges, tangerines and grapefruit
- kumquats
- coconuts
- beetroot

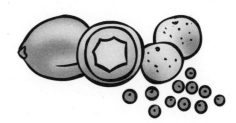

132. Impervious fruit and vegetables?

If you can't buy organic – for reasons of either budget or availability – know where exactly to compromise.

- Any fruit that is thick-skinned and will definitely be peeled (loose-skinned clementines, satsumas, kiwi fruit, bananas) will have less pesticide in the edible parts than a thinner-skinned fruit, especially one you might eat whole (such as an apple).
- Contrast the vulnerable vegetables in Tip 133.
- Anything oily, such as nuts, even if peeled or shelled, is more likely to hold on to chemical residues.
- If you're going to zest citrus fruit, do make sure it is organic.

133. Pesticide pains

What you should buy organic, because they are more likely to be heavily sprayed and/or more likely to hang on to residues:

- peaches and similar stone fruits (apricots, plums, nectarines), both fresh and dried
- berries (strawberries, raspberries)
- apples and pears
- grapes, raisins and sultanas
- cherries
- lemons and limes (because you don't usually peel before serving)
- tomatoes
- potatoes
- celery and leafy greens, including salad leaves and spinach

- cucumbers
- chillies and sweet peppers
- French and runner beans
- carrots
- courgettes and other squashes
- mushrooms

134. Organically ugly?

If you're choosing to buy organic, note that your shopping bag possibly won't look as good as with regular produce!

- Expect produce to look anything but pristine!
- Organically grown vegetables, especially heirloom varieties, will not necessarily have the regular shape, large size and glossy skin of conventional farm produce. Most of the latter are bred for looks, and may have been genetically modified or surface treated to make them more attractive.
- Don't be alarmed by holes in leafy greens – it's most likely safe as long as you wash them well and cook correctly. Even an apple with a worm hole near the stem may not be bad eating – cut and core, and you will probably find that most of the fruit is sound.

135. Poor picks

Organic or not, there are warning signs for all produce:

- Any fruit or vegetables contaminated with mud or soil, must be washed thoroughly before use to avoid the risk of E. coli infection.
- Always wash your hands after handling muddy fruit or vegetables to avoid cross-contamination.

Basic Techniques and Standby Staples

This chapter provides preliminary preparation how-tos, including time-saving and trouble-saving hints, ingredient substitutions and larder stocking tips.

■ Preparing fruit and veg

136. No more tears

Stop crying over chopped onions.

- Halve and drop them in a bowl of cold tap water. Leave for 5 minutes before you peel, slice or dice to reduce the pungency. As a bonus, the soggy skin will slip off easily.
- If you're short of time, rinsing the onions under running water for a few minutes will also help.

137. Skinned shallots

Although small, these tiny flavourful onions can also reduce you to tears.

- Top and tail the shallots and drop into boiling water.
- Leave to stand for a minute, then drain.
- Gentle pressure from the fingers should pop the shallot out of its skin!

138. Slicing avocado smoothly

Soft, creamy avocado flesh is easily mushed up – trying to peel and slice is almost always a bad idea.

- Instead, halve and slice while still in the skin (it's tough enough not to break if you go lightly).
- Scoop out the end piece with a spoon, and the others should slide out easily with the slightest nudge of a blunt-tipped paring knife.

139. Peeling ginger? Blunt is best

The knobbly shape of ginger coupled with its thin, papery skin means neither a paring knife nor a peeler will make a clean breast of it – plus you'll lose precious chunks.

- Use the edge of a teaspoon; the curved shape helps it get into the crevices more readily.

140. Dipping Mr Potatohead

When you have a large pile of spuds to peel or cut up, sit down with a big bowl of cold water.

- Drop the peeled or diced potatoes in the water as you work to prevent discoloration.

142. Criss-cross crisps

If you have a mandolin with a 'crinkle cut' slicing blade, you can get 'basketweave' potato crisps.

- Take the first slice off and discard to leave a ridged surface on the potato.
- Now turn it through a right angle for the next slice – it will have a perforated hatched pattern.
- Continue slicing, turning the potato 90° for every slice.
- Rinse off the surface starch and dry carefully on kitchen paper before deep-frying.

141. Grate – No peel!

Don't peel if you don't have to!

- Leave the peel on potatoes, sweet potatoes or carrots that you intend to grate.
- It won't interfere except to add the subtlest hint of texture to carrot cakes or rösti-style potato pancakes.

143. Okra on top

The sap inside okra pods acts as a thickener in gumbos. It also makes chopped okra a difficult vegetable to cook, since it gets gluey before starting to crisp up unless deep-fried. However, if you have tender baby okra pods, consider cooking them whole so as not to release the sap and retain all the moisture.

- Carefully trim the top of the stem end, taking off just enough to not puncture the pod through to the hollow core. No leaking sap!
- Of course, you'll have to make sure the tip at the other end is sound too.

144. Seedless pepper

The quickest way to de-seed a pepper:

- Cut in half vertically, along the pepper's natural grooves on opposite sides of the stem.
- Twist gently to separate the halves. The main cluster of seeds under the stem will come away with one half.
- Grasping the stem and seed bundle with your fingers, gently rock to loosen and pull away from the pepper.
- Place the halves face down on a chopping board and tap sharply to loosen any clinging seeds inside so they fall out.
- Finally, trim away any white membranes along the ridges with your paring knife.

145. Pumpkin peeler

If you need your pumpkin peeled and diced for sautéing to add to a stew or soup, cut it before you peel it.

- Whether Halloween monster pumpkin or slender, shapely butternut squash, first slice it up – preferably widthwise, so that you get cross sections with seeds in the middle.
- This may not be practical for a big pumpkin, so cut that into wedges instead.
- Now sit the circles of squash flat and trim off the peel by cutting 'facets' off the rim.
- Halve each circle and scoop out the seeds, then dice.
- For the vertical wedges, first dice so you can lay them on their sides in flat arcs, and peel as described above.

146. Clean greens

Washing salad leaves or other leafy greens?

- Forget the colander – grit that gets moved by the splashing water too easily resettles in the crevices of the leaves.
- Instead, fill a large bowl with clean cold water and plunge the leaves in, pumping up and down or swishing around by hand to rinse.
- Lift out and empty the water – the grit should have fallen to the bottom – and repeat twice.
- Shake off excess water using a salad spinner (yes, you can shake by hand and then pat dry each leaf, but this is so much faster!).

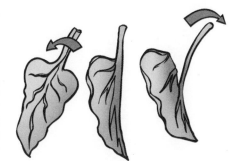

147. De-veining greens

Most greens are better off without the tough central vein. Remove stem and main vein from spinach, sorrel, mustard, radish and kale in one go:

- Fold each leaf along the central vein, glossy upper surfaces inwards.
- Hold them by the leaf margins with the central vein on top.
- Grasping the end of the stem, pull up and away to 'peel off' the central vein from the leaf.
- Cut away brittle lettuce stems before you shred the leaves.

148. Best face forward

When it comes to tight-headed greens such as lettuce, endive and even firm cabbage, many of the nutrients are actually in the outer leaves that see more sun.

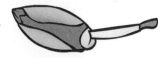

- Try not to lose those outer layers, provided they are smooth, glossy and undamaged.

- On the other hand, the stems of lettuce aren't very tasty and the core of the Belgian endive can be positively bitter. Cut those away before you shred the leaves.

149. Cut to the core

Preparing cruciferous vegetables:

- For cabbages, core as you would a Belgian endive. Unlike bitter endive hearts, cabbage stems are good to eat, though, so shred into the dish a little earlier than the leaves!
- Cauliflower cores are tougher, but you can slice tender parts finely and cook with the florets.
- With broccoli, the skin is tougher – you can keep tender stems after peeling. Slice deep into the stems to help them cook faster (broccoli florets are more tender than cauliflower).
- Cut a cross in the base of Brussels sprouts.

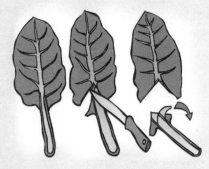

150. Skin the chard

A tough, translucent membrane covers the stalks of Swiss chard. You'll know it's there when the knife slips! But don't wait for accidents to happen.

- Lay each leaf flat, concave surface of the stem upwards, and make a v-shaped incision into the leaf to take out as much of the flat white (or coloured) stalk as possible.
- Cut off the pointed tip of the stalk, but don't cut all the way through the outer membrane. Use the 'tab' top to pull it away, down the length of the stalk.
- Now you can cut it into pieces and cook.

151. Greek stuffed leaves

Dolmades can be made by wrapping a stuffing of rice in cabbage or vine leaves. To make tight, secure parcels:

- Place a spoonful of stuffing near the base of a leaf.
- Fold the bottom edge over the stuffing, then fold the sides inwards over it.
- Roll from the bottom up.
- Cook with the seam downwards.

152. The whole tamale

Yet another leaf wrap, this way of rolling a tamale is easier still than dolmades (*see Tip 151*) and requires no string.

- Place two parboiled corn husks on top of each other, oriented at right angles to each other to make a cross shape.
- Spoon stuffing into the centre – at the crux of the cross.
- Fold as with the dolmades – bottom first, then sides (that is, the ends of the second husk) and finally roll to take up the top.

153. The simplest sorbets

Universally appealing, a refreshing fruit sorbet is so easy to make it should become a freezer staple. The only problem is stopping yourself polishing it off in one go!

- Any juice can be sweetened and chilled – syrup made with about 200 g/7 oz sugar in 300 ml/ 10 fl oz water mixed with 600 ml/1 pint of juice is perfect for a citrus, berry or grape sorbet.
- For naturally sweeter fruit such as peaches, just dilute the juice to taste.
- Leave it to freeze solid and scrape up to serve as a pebbly granita, or wait until it's slushy and beat again for a smoother texture.
- Once it sets smooth again, fold in a stiffly beaten egg white during a second whisking for a creamier sorbet.
- You can also add some chopped fruit, herbs or zest at this point, but don't overdo it.

154. Simple sauce for stuffed pasta

- A herbed butter is the easiest thing to toss with some freshly cooked ravioli (*see Tip 190*).
- Add quickly sautéed garlic – do not brown – and fresh herbs if you have some to hand to pep it up.
- A scattering of snipped sun-dried tomatoes would also be good.

■ Store cupboard standbys

155. Larder-aged liqueur

You'll need to lock this up for a week at least to get the flavours going. It will, however, keep for 3 months.

- Thaw 700 g / 1 lb 9 oz frozen blueberries, raspberries or currants and mash with a fork.
- Stir in a bottle of white wine.
- Cover with clingfilm and leave to steep in the fridge for 3 days.
- Sweeten with 450 g / 1 lb of caster sugar and perhaps a couple of spoonfuls of Cointreau or white crème de menthe.
- Strain and bottle.
- Serve cold in shot glasses or top up with sparkling wine in a flute.

156. Melon in a bottle

You can get fancy with the added flavours, but the simplest preserves are just sugar and fruit. Melon jam is the easiest to make.

- Cube your melons – whether cantaloupe, honeydew or musk melon (anything but watermelon will work).
- Place in a large flat dish with enough sugar to cover.
- Refrigerate overnight.
- In the morning you'll find a slush in the dish! If it's too runny to spoon up easily, simmer till just thick enough and bottle in sterilized jars (*see Tip 14*).

157. Adaptable apricots

Dried apricots – the leathery hard ones with the stones in, not the plump ready-to-eat sort – have a considerable shelf life. Indeed, they could put any prune to shame!

- Soak them in enough hot water to cover, with a few points of star anise.
- Leave overnight. By morning, they will have swelled and softened.
- Now remove the stones and blend the fruit, with just enough of the liquid to render a sticky paste.
- Bottle in sterilized jars (*see Tip 14*) and serve with bread and cheese.

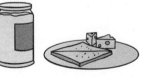

158. Mayonnaise made easy

Preparing your own mayonnaise is well worth the effort. For the lightest, smoothest results, follow the three golden rules:

- Start with all the ingredients (eggs, oil, mustard and vinegar) at cool room temperature – if they're either too cold or too warm you'll end up sorting out a curdle.
- Add the oil in a slow stream, whisking constantly.
- If you do end up with a curdled sauce, add a teaspoon of cold water and whisk again. Otherwise, another egg yolk added in might help.

159. Versatile vanilla!

Vanilla pods may seem expensive, but they have a long and very useful life!

- Once you've scraped the vanilla seeds into a custard, what is left of the vanilla pod can be snipped in two and kept in a jar of sugar for a couple of months to lend its flavour.
- And it's still got some life left in it! Now you can whiz up the pod with some caster sugar for a second speckled batch.
- The first batch is good for adding just a hint of flavour – for sprinkling on fruit or stirring into your coffee.
- Use the second batch in batters and doughs for a more intense finish and a pretty, speckled effect – not very different from the seed scrapings!

160. Radiant dried herbs

An alternative method for drying your own herbs uses the microwave oven.

- Wash the herbs and pat dry with a tea towel.
- Sandwich between two layers of sturdy kitchen paper and microwave on high, turning every minute, until dry.
- Herbs dried by this method will stay looking vibrant – they don't fade as much as the air-dried kind.

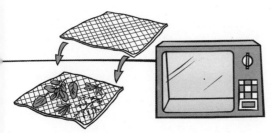

161. Vinegar variety

Make your own flavoured vinegar.

- Use rice vinegar with Asian herbs (lemongrass, galangal, Thai basil); white wine vinegar for European herbs; cider vinegar with spices.
- For 300 ml/10 fl oz vinegar, use a handful of herbs or 2 tablespoons of spice, pounded or crushed lightly.
- Stronger flavours (ginger, basil) infuse in a week. Subtler herbs (marjoram, tarragon) need two weeks.
- Strain into sterilized bottles. Add a few whole spices or herb sprigs to identify.
- Use within six months.
- If it's a fleshy ingredient (chilli, ginger, lemongrass, mint), refrigerate. Otherwise a cool, dark cabinet is fine.

163. *Vodka vroom!*

As with vinegar (*see Tip 161*), so with vodka – creating your own cabinet of flavours is both easy and impressive.

- Use a handful of spices or herbs, perhaps even a couple of spoons of fruits (berries give beautiful colour) for a single bottle.
- Steep for at least two weeks.
- Colour will be leached from the ingredients, so strain and add some of the fresh ingredient once well flavoured.
- Keep chilled and serve very cold – from a packed ice bucket – for thick, syrupy shots.
- If you like, rim shot glasses with a coordinating infused sugar or flavoured salt – vanilla with cinnamon sugar, chilli vodka with celery salt, citrus with pepper.
- You can infuse brandy, rum and other spirits in a similar fashion.

162. *Aromatic oils*

Make your own:

- Refined olive oil and rapeseed oil make the best bases.
- Flavour with spices, seeds, nuts, herbs, onion or garlic, wild mushrooms or nuts.
- Dried ingredients are best; moisture from fresh ingredients hastens spoilage.
- Add 2 tablespoons of robust flavouring (or 4 tablespoons of mild) to 450 ml/16 fl oz oil.
- Heat in an oven at 150°C/300°F/Gas Mark 2 for 1 hour 40 minutes. The oil must reach 120°C/250°F (check with a sugar boiling thermometer).
- Strain and bottle, leaving minimal air between oil and cork.
- Use within a month.
- Think sweet too – angelica, vanilla, citrus peel, fennel, saffron and nut oils are excellent with desserts!

164. Trouble-shooting

A couple of odd things can happen when you make your own flavoured oil, vinegar and liqueurs.

- Sometimes the flavoured oil becomes cloudy – this indicates there is moisture present (from the flavouring ingredient). Pour out into a tin, reheat until the cloudiness disappears and rebottle from scratch.
- Many of your flavourings will tend to float into the neck of the bottle. As you use the liquid, longer stalks of herbs or chillies become more exposed. This contact with air can make them spoil, so either use up within a week of opening, or top up the liquid to cover the flavouring ingredient. (This dilutes the flavour slightly, but if you're using the liquid slowly, it will soon catch up – particularly in the case of vinegar or vodka.)

165. Extra special sugar (or salt)

Infuse your own sugar or salt:

- Blitz sea salt or sugar in a blender with pepper, garlic, citrus peel or vanilla pods for the most intense flavour.
- You can get a good flavour over time by lightly bruising the ingredient (vanilla, garlic, chillies, celery or cinnamon) and placing in a jar of salt or sugar. This is useful for large amounts – sugar you intend to bake with or salt to be used as a 'crust' on meat or fish.
- There's little danger of spoilage as both sugar and salt 'pickle' the flavouring ingredient.

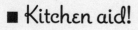

■ Kitchen aid!

166. Low-fat spray

Make your own oil spray or mister for low-fat frying.

- Simply mix equal amounts of vegetable oil and water in a clean household-standard spray bottle and shake well.
- Experiment with different oils and ratios of water-to-oil to find what works best for you in terms of flavour and ease of cooking.
- You will need to clean the nozzle of the bottle regularly to prevent clogging. A baking powder solution sprayed through it should do the trick.

167. Clogged sauce bottle?

Got a bottle of ketchup that won't deliver?

- Put the cap on and thump the bottle firmly (but not too aggressively!) on the worktop a couple of times.
- If the sauce has congealed, try pushing a fat straw in and out – that should mix it up nicely as well as let air in (in case a blockage at the neck has 'bottled' it in!).
- If it's really stiff, try adding a small drip of oil and shake to loosen. Do not add water, as this could hasten spoilage.

168. Locked in place

Jars refusing to unscrew?

- Get a (better) grip. A flat rubber band slipped around the circumference of the lid can help.
- Leave the jar in the refrigerator for 10 minutes; remove and run hot water over the lid before you try again.
- Try using a small screwdriver to carefully ease the lid away from the jar – it may break the vacuum. (Replace the mangled lid or decant the contents later.)

■ Less mess, more speed

169. Bag your books

Cookbooks are great, but trying to keep them open at the right page while you follow a recipe can be a nightmare!

- Put your cookbook, opened to the correct recipe, in a clear plastic folder or bag to protect it from smears and splashes as well as keeping the pages from falling shut or flipping in a breeze.

170. Sticky measures

About to measure out sticky stuff like honey, treacle, peanut butter or jam?

- Grease your measuring spoons and cups lightly first, and the ingredients will slip off more easily.

171. It's a wrap!

Avoid getting sticky, greasy hands, rolling pin and worktop dirty from buttery or crumbly pastry, dough, marzipan, even ready-roll icing. Keep the mess under wraps!

- Use either a large polythene bag cut up along one side to resemble a folder or two sheets of greaseproof paper to make the wrap.
- Lay the bag or a sheet of the paper on the worktop. Place your dough on this – centred on the paper or in one half of the bag.
- Lay the other sheet of paper on top or fold the other half of the bag over to enclose the dough.
- Roll as usual. When you need to peel the dough off the worktop, simply lift the paper or plastic!

172. A drop of colour or flavour

Adding flavour concentrates, artificial flavourings or food colouring to a dish? We know all brands aren't made equal – the cookbook's ½ teaspoon may be too much or too little unless your brands match!

- Use a medicine dropper (available at pharmacies) to add the liquid a drop at a time, mixing and checking as you go. It can make all the difference between an appetizing lime green icing and full-on monster goo!

173. Coppered eggs

There is one exception to the rule that you should never prepare, cook or serve foods in unlined copper vessels.

- A round-bottomed all-copper bowl will drastically reduce the elbow grease you need to whisk egg whites!

174. Easy egg-shelling

Shelling hot boiled eggs will often bring away chunks of the white, giving you an untidy result.

- Plunge boiled eggs straight into cold water. This loosens the hold of the shell on the white, so it comes away readily.

175. Eggy garnish

Chopping hard-boiled eggs really small for a salad or garnish gives very appetizing results, but can turn into a chore when cooking for a crowd.

- Give the knife a rest and press the eggs through a metal mesh sieve (the one you use for straining soups) for a pretty mimosa finish on green vegetables.

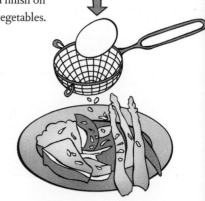

176. Cleaner grater

You couldn't do without your handy box grater. What you certainly could do without is teasing bits of vegetable or cheese out of the holes!

- Unless you're working with something very slippery, add a light coat of oil to the grater. Wipe an oil-moistened tissue down the face or spritz with cooking spray.
- When it's time to clean up, use a baby toothbrush instead of your usual dishwashing brush.

177. Steep the saffron

Saffron is an expensive spice, so you really need to treat it with respect.

- Never add saffron, even crumbled, directly to a dish – you risk making it bitter.
- Soak a few threads of saffron in warm water or milk – not stock! – for about 10 minutes for best results.
- If you need more than a few stamens of this spice (such as the ½ teaspoon some 4-serving recipes call for!), it's time you started shopping around for a cheaper brand.
- Try switching your supply source – go to an ethnic grocery (Indian or Middle Eastern) where it moves off the shelves faster.

178. Bountiful bay!

A few leaves of fresh bay can make a
fantastic and unexpected addition to
a range of dishes.

- Thread some on skewers, interleaved with
  vegetables, for barbecuing.
- Tuck a few into pots of cold orange soufflé
  or ice cream.
- Fresh bay adds a lovely depth of flavour to
  plain bread sauce.
- A wreath of bay placed on a cake that is intended
  to mature slowly will bring out the flavours of
  winter spices and preserved fruit.

179. Limey tang

Don't discard the peels after squeezing
lime juice! Make a substitute for Moroccan-
style preserved lemons, lovely in roasts
and tagines:

- Start with the juice and squeezed halves of one
  lime in a pickling jar, plus a teaspoon of salt.
- Continue adding squeezed limes and a sprinkle
  of salt.
- When the bottle's full, give it a vigorous shake
  and add olive or canola oil to just cover.
- The pickle will be ready to eat in 2 weeks.
- You can pickle whole limes too – layer slices with
  salt and chilli, then top up with oil.

■ Smart swaps

180. Milk and water

Some recipes call for evaporated milk to be diluted to the consistency of whole milk.

- To achieve the right consistency add an equal volume of water.

181. Low-fat cream

An all-natural alternative to whipped cream with lots more nutrition for far less fat:

- Just whisk up a can of evaporated milk. It won't hold its fluffy shape for long though, so serve at once.
- Get lovely stiff peaks by chilling the can well and whisking in a chilled metal bowl.

182. Low-salt savory

Savory, an old-fashioned herb available in both winter and summer forms, isn't seen often these days. However, it is worth searching out at the farmers' markets for its unusual piquancy.

- Sharp savory makes a good substitute for salt and will be appreciated by those on low-sodium diets.
- Winter savory is more pungent than the summer herb, so use judiciously.
- Savory is very good with legumes – it has even been called the 'bean herb'.

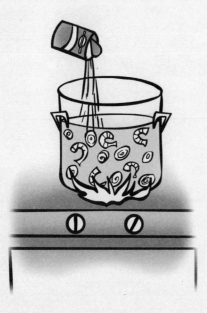

183. A fishy alternative

It's not always easy to keep a supply of fish stock in stock.

- A good substitute is clam juice from a can. Chances are the clams themselves wouldn't look out of place in that stew you're making either!

184. No nam pla?

Here's an easy substitute for Asian fish sauce, nam pla.

- For a tablespoon of nam pla, use 2 teaspoons soy sauce and a teaspoon of mashed anchovies for a very similar salty fish taste.

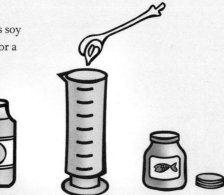

185. Pesto to the rescue!

Yes, we know pesto is traditionally made with basil and pine kernels. However, an adventurous multi-herb pesto can use up the few sprigs of herbs lingering in the vegetable drawer.

- Taste your mix after adding the nuts, garlic and oil to see if the flavours are intense enough. If not, you can add a piquant extra such as tapenade or sunblush tomatoes, or even a jalapeño chilli!

186. Hot stuff!

Ever wondered how much the heat of a hot pepper sauce compares with that of a whole chilli?

- Well, about ½ teaspoon of standard powdered red chilli would substitute for 16 drops of Tabasco sauce, so a single drop is about the same as $\frac{1}{32}$ teaspoon of chilli powder.
- This is only a rough guide – there are several varieties of chilli peppers that are hotter or milder than the 'average' ancho chillies.

187. Beat the brown

Run out of brown sugar? You can mock up your own if you have some molasses.

- For 280 g/10 oz brown sugar, mix a tablespoon of thick dark molasses into 225 g/8 oz plain sugar!

■ As easy as that!

188. No-cook carbs

When you're too tired even to bake a potato or don't have any bread at home, try opening a can of beans for a change.

- Add some chopped salad veggies (tomatoes, onions and parsley are easiest) and serve a grilled chicken breast on a bed of beans.
- These could be a substitute for mashed or boiled potatoes, and are more interesting in terms of texture and taste.

 =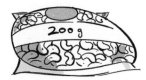

189. Dried legumes for canned

Whether it's chickpeas, haricot or kidney beans – or any other pulses, really – the substitution rule is that approximately half the can weight equals the dry weight needed.

So if your recipe calls for a 400 g/14 oz can, soak a little over 200 g/7 oz dried beans overnight and cook till tender.

190. Ravioli wrappers!

You can still enjoy homemade ravioli or tortellini without a pasta machine. It's a bit of a cheat in terms of the dough, though…

• Use wanton wrappers instead of pasta dough to sandwich your fillings. Then brush the edges with a little water before either scoring together with a fork or crimping shut by hand.

Cooking
On the hob, in the microwave

'Meals in minutes', recipe hints, secrets from the pros, common errors and salvaging failures, simple garnishes and serving suggestions – even no cook dishes; plus a section on making the most of your microwave oven.

■ **Chef's confidential**

191. Catch the bouquet!

It's easy to lose sight of that little muslin bag of herbs in your big stockpot, and fishing through it ladleful by ladleful is oh-so-frustrating!

- Use a long string to tie the bouquet garni and knot its other end round the handle of your stockpot. Now all you have to do is tug to retrieve!

192. Bouquet épicerie?

Yes, you use a bouquet garni for a bunch of herbs. But how do you deal with smaller seeds and berries and crumbled dried herbs?

* Tie them in a muslin bag – this will let you crush them with the back of the spoon to release flavours – or use a tea ball, if you have one. Beats chasing after every peppercorn and clove to discard later!

193. Dried in first, fresh in last

For maximum flavour, the same herbs should be added to dishes at different times, depending on whether they are fresh or dried:

* Dried herbs usually need to steep a bit – crumble and add early on, at the sautéing or sweating stage, or when marinating.
* Fresh herbs are more delicate and aromatic – bruise lightly or tear and add towards the end of cooking.
* Woodier-stemmed herbs can go in earlier than soft-stemmed ones, even at the start of a quick-cooking recipe.
* Dried herbs used in a rub can stay in when grilling or barbecuing.
* Marinades with fresh herbs will burn and blacken unless kept moist during cooking by basting or braising.

194. Sweat while you sauté

When sweating vegetables do make sure they soften before browning. This will help the flavours to blend better.

- If you're using a heavy-based pan – which should mean your vegetables won't catch as easily during frying – put the lid on while you sauté, only uncovering to stir occasionally.

195. Cold water or hot?

When making stew or simmering a soup, you will often find recipes telling you to add hot stock to the sautéed vegetables.

- Cold water or stock will reduce the temperature in the pot, lengthening the cooking time.
- However, if you don't mind the wait, cold water will actually draw out the flavours better.

196. Hot or cold soup?

Some soups, such as vichyssoise, can be served either hot or cold, but it's important to decide how you'll be serving yours before you start cooking.

- The seasoning has to be more emphatic with a chilled soup.
- When soup is served hot you can have a lighter hand with the spices.
- If you really can't decide – or intend to serve the same dish in two separate batches – start with less spice and, when serving cold, stir in some fragrant pesto, a little anchovy paste, or a drizzle of flavoured oil and tapenade.

197. Fat disposal

Pouring hot oil down the sink won't do nice things to your plumbing – in fact, it's one of the fastest recipes for clogged drains.

- Drain the fat into a milk or juice carton with a cap. When cool, replace the cap and dispose of the carton.

■ Cereal comfort

198. Perfect pasta

Keeping a little of the starchy cooking water from pasta will help the sauce cling better!

- Leave a little water in the pan – just a couple of tablespoons – when draining pasta.
- If you're using a colander (or two-part pasta pan), add 3–4 tablespoons of the water when mixing in the sauce.
- Alternatively, instead of using plain water, add a ladleful of the pasta cooking water to the sauce when simmering it. Add salt to taste later – the cooking water will already be salted.

199. Springtime pasta

Cheat yourself into springtime exuberance when winter's overstaying its welcome.

- Add a small bag of frozen baby peas to your pasta for the last 5 minutes of cooking time.
- Drain and season with a little lemon zest and juice, freshly ground white pepper and a sprinkling of Parmesan.

201. *(Almost) No-stir risotto*

Making risotto won't need all that babysitting while you add the stock by the ladleful!

- Measure correctly to begin with. Allow about 1.5 litres/2¾ pints water or stock (total liquid, if using wine as well) for every 300 g/10½ oz risotto rice.
- Add it all to the pan at once, reserving 225 ml/ 8 fl oz to add later if necessary, and bring to a simmer.
- You will need to stir it occasionally to prevent sticking, but it shouldn't need constant attention.
- Stop cooking while the risotto is still slightly runnier than you want the final consistency to be – the starch will 'stiffen' a bit once removed from the heat.

200. *Non-stick steaming*

Making wontons or dumplings in your trusty bamboo steamer? Most of us add a sheet of foil to prevent a soggy, sticky mess at the bottom – but then the dumpling stops being a pot-sticker and sticks to the foil instead!

- Try using a leaf of lettuce, cabbage or spinach for each dumpling instead. They'll slip off readily, and you can always add the leaves to a side dish of soup.

■ Dashing dairy, perfect poultry

202. Buttery barrier

If your hot milk is always boiling over:

- Rub the rim of the saucepan with butter or oil to a depth of up to 2.5 cm/1 inch to prevent the milk boiling right over. It will still froth up, but would need to boil very fiercely indeed to breach the butter barrier.

This also works when cooking pulses and lentils, which tend to froth quite a bit.

203. Perfect poaching

Restaurant-perfect eggs Benedict call for perfectly poached eggs, holding together nicely with no straggles of white streaming out.

- Start with a deeper pan – sauté rather than frying. Break the egg into a saucer or espresso cup. Give the water a whirl with a ladle when it's hot, to form a miniature whirlpool in the centre, and then quickly and gently slide in the egg. The centrifugal force pulls the eggs in neatly!
- For multiple eggs, use a flatter pan. Place round biscuit cutters in the pan so that the water almost reaches the rim but the bubbles can't quite break over. When the water's hot, break the eggs into their individual biscuit-cutter bastions.

204. Softly scrambled

Problems getting your scrambled eggs right?

- For soft scrambled eggs that are cooked through but not rubbery firm, mix a tablespoon of natural yogurt into every 4 eggs.

■ Fine fish (and flesh)

205. 'Blackened' bream, or bass, or...

Cajun-style blackened fish gets its flavour from a spice mix that's now easy to buy at any supermarket. Its charred appearance, however, is a spot of culinary deception.

- Do not overcook the fish to 'char' it!
- Instead, dip the fish pieces in melted butter and then press on a plate of the seasoning mix to coat.
- Heat a cast-iron griddle to a high temperature – a drop of water should sizzle on the surface – without any oil.
- Now sear the fish directly on the dry griddle for about 2 minutes on each side, until it looks lightly charred.

206. Slash and grill

When searing or griddling meat and fish, here's how to prevent it 'curling' as it cooks:

- Cut a few diagonal slashes in the flesh – on both sides for a cut of meat and on the skin side for fish. For sausages, a few good pokes through the casing should do it.
- While cooking, use your spatula or fish slice to press the fillet or cut down lightly against the pan to help it cook evenly.
- For very tender cuts of meat such as veal escalopes, instead of slashing, just score the flesh lightly with the back of a heavy cleaver or knife.

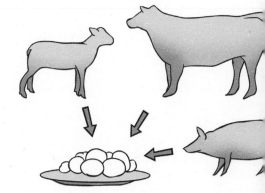

207. Meatball medley

To deepen the depth of flavour in dishes using chopped or minced meat, divide and double up!

- For meatballs and sauces for pasta, consider using a blend of lamb or beef and pork mince.
- You can do the same for pies, casseroles and terrines.
- For fish, which cooks faster, add a cured meat – try a little chopped ham in a seafood mould, for instance.
- However, don't try this with dishes that require only brief cooking – burgers, for instance – as not all meats cook at the same rate.

208. For the juiciest burger

For burgers that stay moist even when well done:

- Provided the weather is cool and you're not cooking outdoors, allow the mince to rest outside the refrigerator for up to an hour. (Don't do this in hot weather, though, as the risk of bacteria multiplying is too great.)
- While making up the burgers, mix in a tablespoon of ricotta cheese, soft cottage cheese, or apple sauce, into each burger.

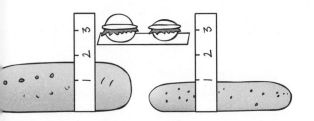

209. Fat or rare?

How thick should your burger be? Well, rather than aesthetics, you should rely on physics.

- If you intend to cook it rare, a thickness of as much as 5 cm/2 inches is fine.
- If you want it well done, though, a burger that thick will dry out and get crumbly on the outside before the inside is cooked. It should be about 2.5 cm/1 inch thick.

■ Valuable tips for vegetables

210. Mash made moreish

This is a good way to sneak vegetables onto the plates of picky eaters.

- First, replace about a third to a half of the potatoes with turnips, celeriac, swede and/or carrots.
- You can boil them in the same pot with the potatoes, adding more tender veg later (baby carrots and young turnips don't need long cooking.)
- Beetroot are nice too, but the colour will be a dead giveaway, so avoid them if you're trying for camouflage!
- Add even more flavour with a little grated nutmeg, a dab of tomato paste or some chopped herbs (rosemary and parsley are both good partners for potatoes).
- Leave it in the refrigerator overnight.
- When you're ready to serve, use a good, fruity olive oil to loosen the mash after reheating.

211. White as a cauliflower...?

Cauliflower can go a bit yellow during cooking.

- To keep the head snow-white as you boil it, add about 200 ml/7 fl oz milk to the cooking water and then pop the cauliflower in head downwards.

212. Best cream of vegetable

Forget the floury roux and the dollops of cream that were once used to give a smooth soup body!

- The easiest method is to add some creamed rice or potatoes, and adjust the seasoning – both kinds of starch tend to soak up the salt in the broth.
- Otherwise use a milder non-tuber vegetable – mushrooms offer a rich flavour boost as well, but caramelized onions, roasted pumpkins and 'melted' leeks all work brilliantly when puréed in the blender.

213. Enokitake

The flavour of most mushrooms intensifies when they are dried or fried. The one exception is the long-legged spidery enoki mushroom. This crisp fungus is nicest raw and cooking for anything more than seconds compromises its delicately sweet flavour.

- Add them towards the end of cooking as you would a garnish of fresh herbs. Or simply sprinkle them on to your salad like any crisp vegetable.

■ Timer-tricking 'traditionals'

214. Faster pasta

Cooking tomato sauce from scratch takes time; ready-made pasta sauce is pricey. Find your comfort zone mid-way.

- Roast a whole trayful of tomatoes when you have a few spare minutes and freeze them in small tubs.
- Roast a whole head of garlic and bottle the creamy contents of the cloves.
- While you cook the pasta, grill some well-seasoned sausages.
- Heat some of the frozen tomato mixture with the creamy garlic and some chilli flakes. Stir in some sage and sliced sausages.
- Tip in the pasta and serve with cheese.

215. One-pot pasta

This calls for cooking pasta as though it's risotto!

- Sauté some onions and/or garlic and any dried herbs you want to use. Add the pasta and stir until glistening.
- Again, take a shortcut and strain some canned tomatoes rather than buying passata.
- Add an equal quantity of stock and bring to the boil, seasoning to taste. Cover and cook until the pasta is tender, but still firm to the bite, adding a little more water if the sauce gets too dry before the pasta is done.

Just one pot to clean!

216. Spaghetti shortcuts

Boil the spaghetti in salted water – and cook the other main ingredient at the same time!

- Add some eggs or blanch some baby spinach. Drain and toss it all together with a little ricotta and a grinding of nutmeg.

Dinner is served!

217. Beans and soda?

Sometimes it seems as if those dried beans will never finish cooking!

- Add a small pinch of bicarbonate of soda (also known as baking soda!). This will soften the tough skin and get them cooking faster.

218. Twice as nice!

You can often cook two foods with different cooking times together if all you're doing is boiling or steaming.

- For instance, you can cook most vegetables along with rice and pasta. Just put the vegetables in a colander and sit it on the rim of the boiling saucepan, so that they come just under the water line.
- The more tender vegetables, such as spinach, broccoli, asparagus or peas, should be balanced just above the level of the water.
- Cook some prawns or mussels the same way on that boiling pot of soup or stock.
- Or boil some eggs to keep in the fridge for later!

219. Asparagus soldiers

An elegant supper doesn't get any easier. Make sure you have plenty of crusty bread to go with it.

- Blanch the asparagus spears and simply serve with a runny egg to dip into, with a few curls of Parma ham and some shavings of pecorino cheese for company.
- Or dispense with the ham and cheese; drizzle over a little truffle oil instead.

Wine with that?

220. Meat, veg — and sauce too

A well-rounded meal needn't mean slaving over the stove all evening.

- Microwave a bag of mixed vegetables while you grill some pork chops.
- When those are done, add some cream and mustard with a splash of wine to the pan drippings.
- When the sauce is bubbling hot and thick, pour it over the chops and vegetables.

Now wasn't that quick? All griddled or roasted meats will yield a delicious gravy or sauce — some stock or cream to dissolve the drippings, a little seasoning, a touch of wine, and you're set.

221. Pre-curry prawns

These bite-sized appetizers are perfect with beer before a curry dinner.

- Stir-fry peeled prawns with Thai-style sweet chilli sauce and toasted white sesame seeds, adding a handful of curry leaves if available.
- Zap mini poppadoms in the microwave with a sprinkling of water until crisp.
- Lay a prawn on each poppadom with a blob of soured cream, a bit of mango chutney and a pinch of cayenne pepper.
- Serve at once; you can't assemble them beforehand as the poppadoms go soft, but you can prepare prawns and poppadoms separately before guests arrive.

222. Quickest curry

This South-east Asian dish practically cooks itself – all you need to keep an eye on is the rice.

- For the curry, mix a carton of coconut milk with the same quantity of stock, a pinch of sugar and 1–2 tablespoons of Thai curry paste – red, green or yellow: you choose!
- Bring to the boil and add some sliced steak or chicken breast.
- Simmer till tender and add a packet of pre-sliced stir-fry vegetables. Heat through and serve with plain steamed rice.

223. Rapid-fire wok dinner

A simple yet sumptuous supper for those days when you simply have no time!

- Stir-fry some peeled prawns on a high heat with just a single green vegetable, such as broccoli, baby spinach or bok choy, then add some teriyaki, black bean sauce or sweet chilli sauce.

■ It's hardly cooking!

224. Lettuce-leaf wraps

This very quick snack or light lunch relies on ready-roasted chicken.

- Shred the meat, lay it on lettuce leaves, add a little coleslaw (minus the mayonnaise) and a drizzle of sweet chilli sauce. Roll up and secure in a serviette.
- For a lunchbox, pack the filling and leaves separately. Spoon into the 'wrap' and eat taco fashion.

225. Stir-fry and... beans?

Canned beans are not only an easy, inexpensive substitute for potatoes or rice (*see Tip 188*):

- They work as a replacement for noodles, too, in stir-fry recipes.
- However, it helps if you can marinate the beans for half an hour in the sauce or dressing ingredients to let the flavours seep in.

226. Treble the tuna

Canned fish will go further if heated up with lots of extra vegetables. It also reduces their high sodium content.

- The 'stretching' ingredients depend on the kind of fish and seasonings in the can. Tomato goes best with mackerel, herrings wouldn't mind a dollop of crème fraiche instead, while sweetcorn and celery are old friends of tuna.
- First sauté some leeks or onions, some fresh herbs or spices if you like, and the sauce base – tomatoes, stock, orange juice (eerily good with sardines!) or cream. Simmer till bubbling and thick, then stir in the fish.
- A cream sauce from scratch is great with smoked fish such as salmon or kippers too. Serve with toast or toss with pasta.

227. Keep the peel

Not all peelings are for the bin!

- Cauliflower stalks, turnip tops and celery leaves are good additions to the stock pot. Indeed, you can cook, purée and strain them into soup!
- Turnip and radish greens are good braised with a pinch of cumin seeds.
- Broccoli and cauliflower greens are nice in a stir-fry.
- Reserve outer leaves of cabbage for cooking fish – pan-roasting on a leaf prevents sticking.
- Unblemished watermelon rinds make lovely pickles – treat like cucumber.
- Tender butternut and pattypan squash can be eaten skin and all – best baked!
- Drop hard cheese rind into a pot of creamy soup for enhanced flavour.

228. Fresh out of crème fraîche?

- Try soured cream or single cream with a squeeze of lime. However, crème fraîche is made from higher-fat double cream and doesn't curdle on heating; soured cream isn't quite so resilient. So substitute only if your recipe allows you to take the dish off the heat and stir it in at the last minute.
- If you must cook with it, try reducing the heat and using beaten natural yogurt (full-fat or Greek-style) with a spoonful of flour to stabilize. You may need to adjust the seasoning as the yogurt can add tartness.

229. Pour the lemon

Pale white lemon drizzle looks so refreshing on a cake. To get that same tangy-sweet flavour alongside a hot dessert, make this creamy lemon 'custard' super-quick!

- Gently scald some pouring cream.
- Remove from the heat and stir in an equal quantity of lemon curd.
- Whisk and strain into a milk jug to serve with steamed puddings, fruit compôte, warm pies and fresh crêpes.

■ Smooth saves!

230. Smoothie too smooth?

If your breakfast smoothie hasn't got enough 'heft', it could be that the fruits you chose were very juicy and there was nothing fibrous enough (such as peaches or wheatgerm) to give your body sustenance. Kiwis, watermelon and similar fruit with a high water content can cause this problem. Or maybe you just added too much juice or ice?

- Add a frozen banana and blend. This is a good bet when you want your drink chilled, but not icy.

231. De-grease a casserole

It's easy to get rid of the greasy bits on a light soup or stock with a skimmer. But that's not so helpful for more chunky soups (such as a chowder) or for stews, casseroles and curries.

- Plop a large flour tortilla on the surface instead; when it starts to soften, lift it out (don't let it get too soggy!). Most of the surface grease should come away with it, but you can repeat if necessary with a fresh one.

232. Peaches and... yogurt?

A great solution for overripe fruit:

- Place in a saucepan with just enough water to cover or a splash of wine.
- Poach until soft and mushy.
- Stir into yogurt or muesli.

233. Deflated!

Many people avoid fibre in the form of beans or cabbage because of embarrassing flatulence. However, traditional ethnic recipes have long known how to neutralize it.

- For cruciferous vegetables (cabbage, Brussels sprouts, cauliflower), beans or lentils, add a tiny pinch of asafoetida to the cooking liquid.
- If sautéing or stir-frying, add a spoonful of anise, coriander, caraway or cumin seeds, or a little fresh ginger.
- Onion and garlic help as well, and go with most things.
- Many herbs counteract flatulence – dill, oregano, marjoram, thyme, coriander, celery, lemon balm, basil and mint.

■ Microwave mettle

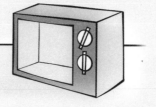

234. Wave, space, density

Different textures of food behave differently in the microwave. And the same food cooks differently based on position!

- Porous, light foods cook faster than dense ones. So bread heats up faster than a potato of similar size or weight.
- If reheating a mixed platter of foods, place denser foods near the edge and the less dense in the centre.
- Juicy foods heat faster than dry. The moist filling of a pie may get hotter than its crust!
- Hot spots are more likely near the edges, so draw food from the periphery towards the centre when stirring.
- For uneven shapes, such as carrots, arrange in a circle alternating thick ends and thin tips. Halfway through cooking, switch tops and tails around.

235. Zap or simmer?

The speed of a microwave is offset by the need to double cooking time when quantity doubles.

- Food for the average family of 4 can be microwaved faster than it can be baked or simmered on the stove. Any more, and it takes as much time or more!
- Any recipe that concentrates flavours by reducing liquid (sauces, stews, soups) takes longer and yields poorer results in the microwave. If you must, start with less water.
- Faster cooking means aromatic ingredients retain more flavour (lost by evaporation in conventional methods). So add a smaller amounts of herbs, spices and garlic.

236. Citrus curd in a zap

Speed up lemon curd in the microwave!

- Combine juice and zest of 1 small lemon, 125 g/4½ oz butter and 100 g/3 ½ oz caster sugar.
- Microwave on full power for 2-3 minutes; stir to dissolve sugar.
- Meanwhile, whisk 3 eggs and strain.
- Add a little of the lemon mixture to the eggs, whisking constantly.
- Now whisk the eggs back into the lemon mixture.
- Microwave for 2 minutes, stirring once or twice.
- Whisk briskly. Stand 2-3 minutes; whisk again.
- Cover with clingfilm and cool before bottling. (If it curdles when eggs are added, a whirl in the food processor while warm renders it smooth.)

Cooking
Baking, grilling, roasting

Tricks for better treats; pointers that take the pain out of pastry; assemblage and presentation maneouvres; recipe rescues; one-dish dinners and barbecue specials.

■ Basic baker's dozen

237. Get a rise out of plain flour

If you run out of self-raising flour just as you're about to get down to a spot of baking, use plain flour – you can add extra baking powder to compensate.

- About a teaspoon for every 125 g/4½ oz flour should do it. Sift thoroughly – maybe even twice for a sponge cake – to distribute well and add lightness.

238. Milk gone sour?

Don't throw out soured milk! Unless it's actually curdled – that is, the whey and solids have separated – it's as good as buttermilk for baking!

- Use in biscuits, breads, scones and pancakes. It's especially effective when you're using bicarbonate of soda rather than baking powder to leaven.

239. Paper or parchment?

Keeping cakes and sweet rolls from sticking calls for a lining of more than grease and flour for foolproof turnouts.

- Silicone bakeware makes it easy – but it's expensive, the options are fewer and you don't want to throw out your old faithfuls.
- Your best bet for baking flat on a tray or sheet is baking parchment – the silicone-coated surface mimics the non-stick properties of silicone baking sheets and has the same flexibility, making for an easy lift-off for scones and biscuits. And no greasing required!
- For lining a tin, though, you're better off with greaseproof paper, but you should brush it with oil to make sure it peels away easily.

240. Think inside the box

Unlike a round cake tin, a rectangular or square baking tin doesn't need to have paper cut separately for base and sides.

- Cut greaseproof paper a couple of inches larger than the tin on all sides.
- Snip diagonally into the corners.
- Grease both tin and paper, and lay the paper in the tin.
- Fold the snipped corners over each other to fit snugly.

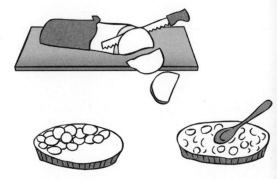

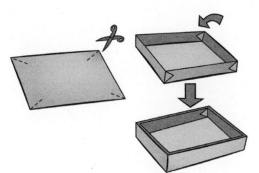

241. Frigid pastry!

If you forgot – or mistimed – the thawing of your ready-to-roll pastry log, you may not be able to make the fancy shapes you wanted.

However, you can still bake a basic open pie or tart shell with it!

- Simply use a sharp knife dipped in hot water to slice rounds of pastry off the log.
- Lay them in the base of the pie dish with the edges slightly overlapping.
- Once you've got it covered, use your fingers to mould the pastry rounds into each other along the 'seams' to finish up with a single 'sheet' – don't worry if it's a bit uneven.
- Blind bake for 3-5 minutes, then add your filling and proceed with your recipe.

242. Heat wise!

These days, we're all looking for energy-saving solutions, so it's time to explode a couple of myths about oven heating.

- You can safely skip preheating the oven for foods that cook slowly over a longer time, such as roast meats, oven-dried tomatoes or baked vegetables.
- You can also switch off the oven a few minutes early, especially when baking at a higher temperature (above 200°C/400°F/Gas Mark 6), if you leave the oven door closed. Obviously, don't do this with more sensitive foods such as soufflés or bread, or when cooking quickly (grilled fish).

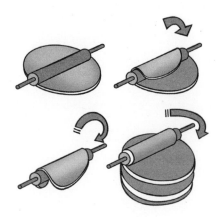

243. Pastry lift

It can be quite a task to lift a round of rolled-out marzipan or sugar paste onto a cake to cover the top. Rolling pin to the rescue!

- Lay the rolling pin down in the middle of the marzipan circle (or square, if that's your shape).
- Pull the end of the sheet furthest from you over the rolling pin, folding it in half.
- Now lift the draped rolling pin, with a gentle half-turn towards yourself as you peel the marzipan upwards.
- To place on the cake, let the nearest end fall on the cake first; then move the rolling pin backwards over the cake to cover, unrolling the flipped-over icing or marzipan to go over.

244. Help for plummeting plums!

Fruits and nuts added to cake batter have a tendency to sink to the base of the tin for all but the heaviest mixes.

- Dredge the fruits with flour and fold gently into the batter last. Do this even for alcohol-soaked fruit.
- The air trapped by the flour will help them 'float' until the cake cooks around them to support their weight!

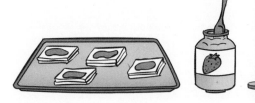

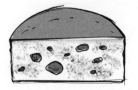

245. Pastry puffs

Left with pastry but no more filling to make a tart or pie?

- You can brush a little preserve or jam on squares of sweet pastry and bake for a quick sweet treat.
- Or brush with fruit juice to glaze and sprinkle on some chocolate chips.
- For savoury pastry, grate some cheese on top for 'open puffs'.
- Or add a layer of pesto, tomato paste or tapenade to flavour more intensely.
- Alternatively, glaze with beaten egg and press in some herbs – chives or tarragon stand up well to the egg.
- Or try a smear of melted butter and a sprinkling of your favourite spice mix.

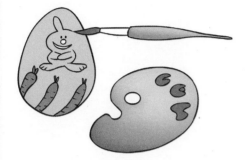

246. Colour me sweet

You can buy coloured icing in a range of shades these days. If you're making your own, though, here are a few pointers.

- All food colouring is very concentrated – add in very small amounts (*see Tip 172*), and mix well before adding more.
- Liquid colour is easiest to work with for pastel shades, for colouring sugar or shreds of desiccated coconut – powder won't mix and paste can obscure the texture – and for painting directly onto rolled-out icing in the pattern you want (make sure your brushes have been used *only* with edible paints!).
- Powder is best if you're after a mottled or marbled effect as it doesn't spread too fast and is easier to control.
- Paste is probably the most versatile. And it's also the best when you want a deep, intense shade.

247. Stop that sliding gâteau!

You've got your three-layers nicely assembled when – horrors! – they begin to slide... Next time, hold them in place with a couple of nifty anchoring techniques.

- If the entire gâteau threatens to leave the platter or cake board, add a blob of royal icing at the base. It will harden as it dries, holding the cake board and lowest layer firmly together.
- If the higher layers are the problem, it could be that they aren't perfectly even – and that's almost a certainty. Use a fork to mark the side of the cake before layering, so you have reference points for lining them up.

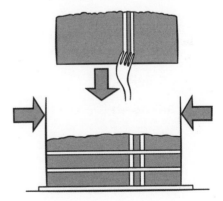

248. No-mess muffins

Muffins – so simple, so versatile, such a comfort. But teasing them out of their tray can be a fiddle. (Not to mention getting the burnt-on dribbles of batter off without bending the cups out of shape!)

You could switch to silicone; but it's pricey and has its own drawbacks (*see Tip 4*). Or you could just put your trust in foil.

- You'll need a sheet about 1½ times the length of your tray.
- Lay it directly on the tray and, starting at one end, scrunch the foil in to line the cups as you go.
- Slip the paper muffin cases in, spoon in the batter and bake.
- When cool, ease up the foil and out pop the cakes!

■ Piecrust promises

249. Nimble pie

It's possible to prepare a pie dinner for four in less than 30 minutes – with leftovers for a packed lunch!

Apart from larder staples, you will need:

- 4 grilled chicken breasts
- 100 g/3½ oz smoked ham or cured bacon
- 140 ml/4½ fl oz cream
- 90 ml/3 fl oz stock
- 250 g/9 oz ready-to-roll puff pastry

Method:

- Preheat the oven to 200°C/400°F/Gas Mark 6.
- Dice the chicken and the ham.
- Mix the chicken with the cream, adding some dried herbs (rosemary or tarragon), the stock, a teaspoon of cornflour and a little mustard powder. Season to taste and pour into a pie dish.
- Roll out the pastry and lay on top, trimming to the rim of the dish. Lightly moisten the edges and press firmly to seal.
- Brush the top with beaten egg for a golden glaze and cook until the pastry is puffed and crisp.

Serve with some blanched haricot beans.

250. Piecrust plight!

Singed pastry case?

- Scoop the filling carefully out of the scorched case and set aside.
- Get a bag of ready-roll piecrust and roll it out – don't worry about getting a neat round or square.
- Lay the pastry on a greased baking sheet and pile the filling in the centre.
- Now simply draw up the pastry 'sides' and scrunch together the edges to close.
- Bake and slice into wedges – think of the irregular shape as rustic chic!

251. Cheat's mince 'pies'

No fiddling with crusts and tart shells!

- Preheat the oven to 200°C/400°F/Gas Mark 6.
- Lightly grease the cups of a mini-muffin pan.
- Cut some filo pastry sheets into squares big enough to lap out of each cup, and line each cup with 2–3 squares. Brush with melted butter. Bake in the preheated oven until golden.
- Mix store-bought mincemeat with an equal quantity of grated apples. Add an extra pinch of cinnamon and a small splash of orange juice if the texture is too dry.
- Plop two spoonfuls into each pastry 'cup' and bake for a further 2–3 minutes.
- Serve with pouring cream or brandy butter.

252. Too cold for warm bread?

A kitchen that's not warm enough won't allow bread dough to rise – not even if you've kept it clear of draughts. This isn't a problem in professional kitchens where they use dedicated proving boxes or cupboards. However, for small quantities of dough you can make do with the microwave oven.

- Bring a large mug of water to boil in the microwave.
- Zap the dough in the microwave for 5–7 seconds on High along with the water.

253. Trusty trick for crusty bread

It can be hard to get that shiny crust on homebaked bread.

- Spritz the inside of your oven with a weak vinegar-water/solution and brush some over the loaf before you quickly shut the door on it.

254. Fresh from the oven, again!

Day-old (or two-day-old) bread in need of a bit of oomph? Here's a trick that'll get it warm, crusty and yeasty fresh again.

- Preheat the oven to 180°C/350°F/Gas Mark 4.
- Spritz the loaf with water and place in the oven for 10 minutes to revive it.

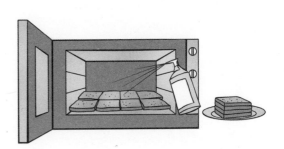

255. Crumbs!

Jazz up fried fish or breaded chicken pieces by adding an extra herby edge to the breadcrumbs.

- Whiz some dry bread in the blender with a small spoonful of herbs.
- Mix in some pepper and salt.
- Coat the meat or fish in the breadcrumbs for a zestier flavour and a fresh green-speckled look.

256. A right roll-up!

Getting the Swiss roll right is just a matter of planning ahead.

- While the cake's in the oven, soak a clean tea towel in hot water and wring out well.
- Lay flat on the worktop with the shorter end facing you.
- Place a sheet of greaseproof paper over the cake tin and turn out the cake, sandwiching the paper between cake and towel.
- Tuck your thumbs under the tea towel and begin lifting it off the counter, rolling up the cake as you 'walk' your fingertips along the back of the Swiss roll to pat and prod the roll firmly into shape!

257. Sunken sponge?

If your sponge cake fell flat, don't waste it, use it to make a gâteau!

- The cake probably isn't as light and airy as it should be, so split it into two or three layers.
- If it looks very dense, soak it in light syrup. If you have a can of fruit, use the liquid from that, or use a sweetened fruit juice.
- Sandwich with some cream cheese flavoured with citrus zest and icing sugar, and slices of fruit.
- Tumble some fruit or frozen berries on top to fill the 'crater'.
- Dust with icing sugar and add a scattering of chocolate shavings or flaked almonds.

258. Tough torte!

Another solution if your sponge hasn't risen or your cake is rock hard:

- Serve a fruit salad. You can use canned fruit heated in water or poach some dried fruits in water with a splash of juice and citrus zest. Top with the diced cake.
- Chop up the cake and serve with a fondue-style hot sauce – melted chocolate, a plain custard or even a thick fruit coulis (especially something naturally sweet, like sieved berries or mangoes).
- Slice the cake into thin slivers and serve with a hot custard swirled with a dessert wine or fruit purée.
- Serve the slivers with a liqueur-infused whipped cream topped with a matching decoration.

259. Carrot cake with a twist!

Substitute one of these equally nutritious vegetables in your carrot cake recipe.

- Grate some sweet potatoes (the orange-fleshed kind), yams or a firm-fleshed pumpkin (or other winter squash).
- With parsnips, the result is subtler and a little nutty.
- Or use something a bit blander, such as apples or courgettes.

■ Cake toppers!

260. Muffin madness

Turn your muffins into a real treat with this rich frosting.

- Mix together 125 g/4½ oz smooth peanut butter with 40 g/1½ oz sifted cocoa.
- Add 200 g/7 oz icing sugar and 100 g/3½ oz redcurrant jam, with just enough single cream to loosen to the consistency you want – you shouldn't need more than 150 ml/5 fl oz.
- Spoon into or pipe onto rich chocolate muffins.

261. No-fuss icing

Dress up store-bought muffins in a jiffy with some chocolate mints (or other individual chocolates).

- Place the chocolate mints on the muffins.
- Place in the microwave oven and cook on High for 15-20 seconds.
- Spread the softened chocolate mint over the top of the muffin and serve.

262. Spoonfuls of swirls

So many recipes tell you to swirl frosting on a cake attractively using a palette knife. Easier said than done!

- Use the palette knife to slather on the icing and then switch to a spoon. Using the back of its 'bowl' prevents you scraping off the icing you've carefully applied!

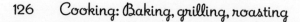

■ Dinner's in the oven!

263. Toads and Yorkies for one

If you're making Yorkshire pudding or toad-in-the-hole for a young family or a special dinner, consider making single-serve portions.

- Oil the holes in a muffin tin and place a spoonful of the batter in each one (with a piece of sausage in each of the 'Toads').

This is far less fiddly than dropping spoonfuls of batter and hoping they hold their shape.

264. Bite-sized 'cannelloni'

Use conchiglie when you run out of the fat cannelloni tubes.

Stuffing the individual shapes may seem fiddly, but they look pretty and are not as messy to eat – which can be a consideration when serving younger children.

- Fill them with diced sausages, curried lentils or sautéed mushrooms or use stuffing recipes which include mince or breadcrumbs.
- Line a shallow dish with the stuffed pasta and bake in a herbed tomato concassé.

Serve with salad, for a smart supper.

265. Speedy spud skewers

Jacket potatoes can seem to take forever to cook! Here's a way of saving as much as 15 minutes' cooking time on a medium potato.

- Push a sturdy metal skewer through the potato before putting it in the oven.

266. Tropical beach jacket potato

Jazz up the humble jacket potato filled with tuna out of a tin, coleslaw and mayonnaise — by upgrading to a more exotic topping.

- Mix together cooked peeled prawns, diced mango or canned pineapple, some soured cream and a little chopped dill.
- Cut a cross on top of a foil-baked barbecued potato, push the sides gently inwards to ease open, and spoon in the topping.
- For an even more luxurious touch, substitute smoked salmon for the prawns, cream cheese for the soured cream, and a couple of capers instead of the fruit. Add a good grinding of white pepper.

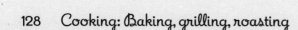

267. Pungent purée

Baked garlic has a surprisingly mellow, buttery flavour. It's worth your while baking several heads at once and refrigerating.

- Wrap 24 whole bulbs of garlic into a single foil package and bake at 180°C/350°F/Gas Mark 4 for about an hour.
- When cool, separate the cloves and gently press – the pod will ooze or slide out readily.
- Purée by passing through a sieve or process with 2 tablespoons of olive oil and some salt.
- Place in a jar and add more oil to cover.
- Refrigerate for up to three months, topping up the oil as you use the purée.
- Use a little on croûtons, in salad dressings and to accompany roasted meats.

268. Whole roast marrow

You don't need to peel, clean and slice medium-sized winter squashes and marrows before cooking. Baking them whole makes them easier to prepare.

- Rub all over with olive oil and bake for approximately 1 hour (or till the skin yields easily to a fork) at 200°C/400°F/Gas Mark 6.
- You don't even need to peel them – just cut them up, discard the seeds and serve, with a drizzle of seasoned soured cream or oil.
- You will have no trouble separating the soft, sweet flesh from the peel with knife and fork.

A nutritious – and different – alternative to jacket or mashed potatoes with a hot casserole or grilled meat.

269. Roasted Mediterranean vegetables

Roasted vegetables needn't be restricted to lazy winter evenings. Try a less starchy selection for a sprightly summer supper.

- Thinly slice some aubergines and dice some courgettes and onion wedges.
- Toss with whole garlic cloves (skin left on).
- Roast for 20-30 minutes at 200°C/400°F/ Gas Mark 6 with a drizzle of olive oil to make a Mediterranean feast.
- A spoonful of balsamic vinegar and a scattering of fresh basil on the vegetables as they leave the oven make them extra special.

270. Quick ham & leek surprise

Choose a dozen very tender baby leeks – or asparagus spears – for this recipe.

- Preheat the oven to 200°C/400°F/Gas Mark 6.
- Wrap a 'sash' of Parma ham around the middle of each leek. Place in a roasting tin, pouring in 125 ml/4 fl oz hot water and a tablespoon of olive oil.
- Roast for 15 minutes or until almost tender.
- Sprinkle over a mixture of breadcrumbs and grated Parmesan.
- Continue to cook until crisp on top.

Serve alone as a starter, or as a side dish with some grilled or poached fish.

271. One-foil fish

Fish cooks quickly; it's usually the vegetables and starchy accompaniments that take more time. Enclosing the vegetables in an airtight packet helps trap the steam in and tenderizes them faster.

- Preheat the oven to 200°C/400°F/Gas Mark 6.
- Construct your own container with a sheet of foil laid on a baking tray.
- Pile some noodles, sliced new potatoes, wedges of sweet potato or some diced pumpkin (or other winter squash) into the sheet of foil.
- Toss in sliced onions or spring onions, green vegetables (beans, broccoli or fennel)*, any herbs or whole spices you want to use, some salt and a drizzle of olive oil.

- Lay the fillet of fish on the vegetables, season well and crimp the edges of the foil square together to close.
- Bake in an oven at 220°C/425°F/Gas Mark 7 for 15-20 minutes (depending on the chosen vegetables and the thickness of your piece of fish).

*If you prefer a more tender green, such as young spinach or asparagus spears, pop them into the packet for the last 5 minutes.

272. Pork & orange rosemary skewers

You know pork goes beautifully with apple sauce or with grilled pineapple. Now try it with oranges.

- Thread diced pork fillet rubbed with salt on rosemary skewers, alternating with chunks of oranges (peel left on).
- Grill or barbecue, basting with orange juice and olive oil.

Serve with a simple bean, red onion and black olive salad dressed with balsamic vinaigrette.

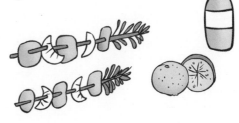

273. Baked wheels of Brie

An interesting turn of the cheeseboard for winter.

- Stuff a whole wheel of mild Brie or Camembert with honey, dates and pecans – just push them into the soft centre. Bake in the oven at 200°C/400°F/Gas Mark 6 until golden and just starting to ooze. Accompany with oat biscuits.
- Insert snipped sun-dried tomatoes into the cheese and smear with pesto. Then parcel up in filo pastry and bake till the crust is done.

274. Not-so-humble crumble

Dinner table trends are now moving away from posh nosh to home bakes with a rustic touch. Fruit crumbles will always be a favourite.

- Dice fruit and macerate with sugar for 10-20 minutes – or as long as it takes to heat the oven to 200°C/400°F/Gas Mark 6 and make the topping.
- How much sugar you use depends on how sweet your fruit is. For instance, tart berries will need more sugar than sweet apples.
- Consider mixing fruits for a colourful result – pale pears and apples get a lovely kick of colour from berries and cherries. Cover with flour rubbed into cold butter till it resembles breadcrumbs and then mix with sugar if your fruit is really tart, or use spoonfuls of rolled oats or muesli sprinkled and dot the top with butter.
- You can add crushed or flaked nuts to the topping, if you like.
- Bake until the top is golden and the fruit is visibly bubbling around the edges.

▪ Bravo – biscuits!

275. Drop the ball

Getting perfect portions of the sticky dough for biscuits on to the baking sheet can be quite a trick – and can result in a headache-inducing number of sticky spoons!

- Get out your small ice-cream scoop, and use the usual method of cold-water dips between drops.

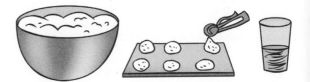

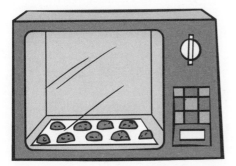

276. Biscuits that crumble!

You baked them chewy, but now those yummy oatmeal-raisin discs have hardened into frisbees.

- Pop them in the microwave for 10 seconds.
- If this doesn't work, brush them with hot milk and place in a cool oven (about 110°C/225°F/Gas Mark ¼) for 5 minutes.
- If you're storing the biscuits in the refrigerator, you might leave a chunk of baked apple in the tin with them to provide some moisture!

■ Barbecue cues

277. Don't shuck the corn

Leave the corn husks on when barbecuing.

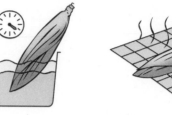

- Soak whole ears, husk and all, in water for 20 minutes before throwing on the barbecue.
- You won't have to worry about soot on the ears or charring.
- Peel back the charred husks, discard and serve – the corn will look as clean as boiled and yet have that smoky barbecue flavour.

278. From freezer to flame

It's great to have frozen burgers or meatballs on hand for a quick dinner, but they spit and stick when you try to brown them in a frying pan.

- Lay them on a baking tray, on the greaseproof paper used to wrap or interleave them.
- Brush with oil and place under the grill to brown.
- When one side is done, switch off the grill and wait for the splatters to subside before removing, turning and basting on the other side. Heat the grill again, and finish cooking.
- Do not attempt to thaw frozen mince or mince products in the microwave if you intend to brown them. This makes them give up their water and become even soggier.

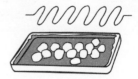

279. Chargrill chequers

Want that restaurant-perfect 'netting' of char marks?

All you need is your ridged griddle pan or your barbecue rack.

- Halfway through the cooking time for each side, pick up the vegetable or meat pieces with tongs and turn them to lie at right angles to their original position.
- Do the same on the other side, and you will have the criss-crossing of char marks on both sides!

280. Soaked satay skewers

Before you make a batch of satay, remember to soak your wooden or bamboo skewers.

- They need to be soaked in water for 10 minutes before cooking to prevent them burning or charring.
- This means that while you can marinate the meat well ahead of time, you shouldn't put them in the fridge pre-skewered.
- Thread the meat on to the soaked skewers just before cooking.

Freezing and Refrigerating

Put precooked foods and partially prepared ones on ice; manage your stocks and garnishes better in the icebox; learn to make your own dips and marinades to have on hand – ready in less time than you need for a grocery run. Pack prettier; thaw without ado; what not to freeze… There's even a superior, no-drinks-dilution trick for ice cubes!

■ Icy cool!

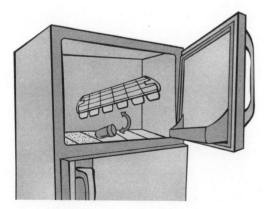

281. Frozen to the spot

If you've ever struggled to lift an ice cube tray out of the freezer:

- Sprinkle some salt onto the metal bottom of the freezer to prevent ice trays from sticking in place.

282. Artful ice

You can add some fun to regular ice cubes even without fancy shaped trays.

- Consider adding citrus twists, olives, capers or maraschino cherries – a nice touch for drinks.
- Non-traditional decorations suspended in ice can add quirkiness to a drink without affecting flavour – sunflower seeds, star anise, yellow pear tomatoes, a knot of liquorice…
- If you are watchful, you can keep an eye on the ice tray until the water is 'slushy', then add a pip of food colouring paste or syrup. It will spread partially if you quick-freeze, giving you Impressionist ice!

283. Nicer than ice!

Ever notice how ice tends to dilute a fruity punch or lemonade, even iced tea, as it melts?

- Keep your beverage at full-strength by freezing diluted fruit juices (half water) in ice trays, then bagging like ice.

When an orange cube melts in your lemonade, you'll call it a cool St Clement's sip!

284. Cold cups

Make your own pretty ice bowls to serve iced desserts on a warm day.

- You'll need two plastic bowls, one a size smaller than the other.
- Suspend the smaller bowl in the larger by taping the rims at 'quarter points' so that they are at the same level (which means the bottom of the small bowl doesn't touch the base of the large one and the gap between the rims is 'bridged' by the sticky tape).
- Add water between the bowls, filling up to 2.5 cm/1 inch from the rim, and freeze.
- To release, pour hot water into the inner bowl and lift it out as soon as it loosens.
- Now briefly plunge the outer bowl in warm water to lift the 'ice bowl' free.

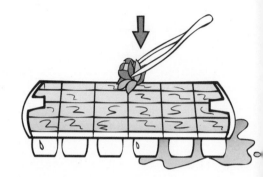

285. Frosted flowers

For desserts and drinks, edible flowers add a lovely twist. Here's a refreshing change from the usual sugar-frosted violets or rose petals.

- Using a tweezer, carefully push the flowers down into the compartments of an ice tray filled with cold water. Freeze to suspend the flower. (This is not very different from the ice garnish trick in Tip 282, but you need to start with chilled water to preserve and embed the blooms properly.)
- You can also use the tweezer to insert flowers or petals between the plastic mould bowls in the 'ice bowl' tip (*see Tip 284*) for a more picturesque serving idea.

■ Preserved in ice

286. Frost-fastened metal

Metal containers withstand freezer temperatures well, and it's a great way to bake from frozen. However, if there's a metal lid as well, chances are it'll freeze fast.

- Try adding a layer of greaseproof paper before putting the lid on. The edges of the paper should stick out beyond the rim.
- If you already have a frosted-up container that needs opening, wring out a tea towel in hot water and wrap around the top to loosen the lid.
- Next time, you might just use a layer of clingfilm followed by foil instead of a lid.

287. Freeze some cream

Cream is not a store-cupboard staple that you can easily hoard. However:

- Thanks to its very high fat content, clotted cream freezes beautifully.

288. Cheese freeze!

If there's more cheese in the refrigerator than you can use over a couple of weeks, it might make sense to freeze it.

- You can freeze most hard cheeses as long as they are full-fat.
- When you thaw it in the refrigerator, wrap in a double thickness of kitchen paper to absorb moisture, then discard the paper and replace with greaseproof paper. Use within a week.
- If you're going to grate the cheese for use in cooking, you can either do so from frozen or grate and freeze in spoonfuls on an open tray, then bag the lumps to use as needed.
- Soft cheeses won't respond well to thawing, so it's better to preserve them in oil. Feta cheese is especially happy to be dunked in olive oil flavoured with herbs and spices – try chilli, cumin, garlic, sage or rosemary for extra flavour.
- You can also shape creamy cheeses such as fresh curd cheese or cottage cheese into balls and keep in oil the same way.
- Camembert and Brie, if not too ripe, freeze magnificently.

289. Frozen-stiff yolks

Eggs can be frozen! As long as you separate whites and yolks, that is.

- If you end up with excess yolks, it's better to freeze them as refrigeration will quickly dry them out (they'll be fine for up to a day if you cover them with cold water) and they will develop a 'skin'. Use within three months.
- Depending on whether you're going to use them in a sweet or savoury recipe, you can sprinkle a little salt or sugar on them before freezing.

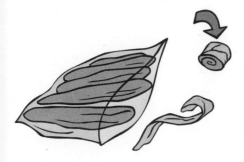

290. Frozen rolled bacon

Yes, like most meats, bacon will keep longer if frozen – and that's good news if you've just bought the economy pack. However, it's almost impossible to peel off a slice of ham or bacon once you've frozen the package.

- Peel each slice off and roll up, then pop into a freezer bag to freeze. Now you can just take out as many as you want to thaw each time.

291. Nutty but nice

Nuts, like flours, will stay fresh longer – most of them for a couple of months – in the refrigerator. However, the freezer is a better bet.

- It can put a stop to any tendency towards rancidness.
- Nuts can be frozen for about a year.
- They won't develop icicles if stored in an airtight container.

292. Mushrooms at their best

Fresh mushrooms should be cooked the day you buy (or pick) them. If you can't do that, freezing is next best – you won't be able to fry them or grill them from frozen, but they'll still be good in a stew or sauce.

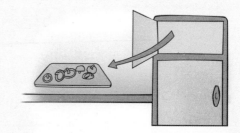

- Firmer varieties withstand freezing better than spongier types – shiitake, chanterelle and closed field mushrooms are better bets than open button mushrooms or soft-stemmed enoki.
- Bring a saucepan of salted water to the boil.
- Line a baking sheet with greaseproof paper.
- Wipe the mushrooms clean of grit with kitchen paper, trim and slice thickly.
- Simmer in the water for 1 minute, then drain.
- Lay out on the baking sheet and open freeze for 30-40 minutes.
- Working quickly, peel off the paper and transfer into a plastic freezer bag; return to freezer.

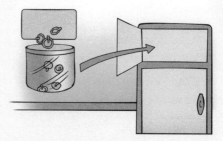

293. Soft fruit? Sorbet!

Berries or stone fruits (such as peaches) looking a little squidgy around the edges?

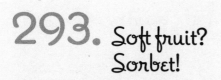

- Purée and freeze them with half the quantity of juice for a quick sorbet or granita.

294. Citrus slices

Orange or lemon glut?

- Freeze the excess for cooking or garnishing.
- Slice thinly and lay in a single layer on a baking tray lined with baking paper to open freeze.
- Peel off carefully and bag to store, arranged one on top of the other like a tower and interleaved with squares of greaseproof paper.
- Use in punches and sangrias straight from frozen.
- Line a cake tin with them for a pretty top (when you upend the cake on a serving platter), layering with a slight overlap before pouring in the cake mixture.
- You can line ramekins or dariole moulds in the same way for steamed puddings.
- Just add to water instead of ice cubes by way of a refreshing summer drink.

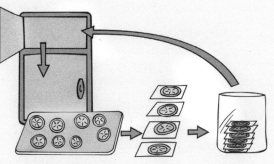

295. Fresh fruit – from the freezer

Hunting down a single piece of citrus fruit just for a recipe can be a pain, so make sure you always have some on hand instead.

- When oranges and lemons are in season, get a large bag of each.
- Zest the fruit and then juice it.
- You can freeze zest and juice separately in ice trays, and then transfer to a bag.
- The juice can be used from frozen in sauces and smoothies (instead of crushed ice, which can dilute fruit flavours).
- The zest can be thawed a cube at a time for flavoured butters and cake mixtures.

296. Easy slushes

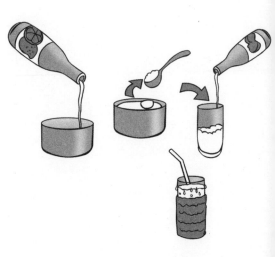

Make use of your freezer to make slushes the easy way:

- Freeze juice – from a single fruit or a blend – until its texture goes grainy, at which point it has legitimately become slush.
- Scoop into glasses, filling halfway, and douse with chilled ginger ale.
- Provide a crochet sleeve for the glasses so the juice doesn't melt from your body heat and insert a straw to sip.

297. Herbs on ice

All too often, half that bunch of fresh soft herbs wilts before you can use it.

- Snip the herbs into small sprigs as soon as you get home, then pop them into ice trays.
- Fill with water and freeze as usual.
- Once frozen, you can pop them out of the tray and bag them in a freezer-safe pouch.

Now you just need to pull out a bag of mint cubes from the freezer to flavour stews, soups, casseroles or lemonade!

298. Sprightly sprigs

Are the herbs in your refrigerator looking a little tired? It's not too late to freeze them, as long as they aren't black or slimy!

- Purée or chop finely and freeze in ice-cube trays – pack them in tightly, and there should be no need to add water. Use in soups and stews.
- Make a sauce by heating with cream and seasoning to taste.
- Rub on joints for roasting, along with some crushed garlic, lemon juice and salt.
- Use wilting herbs for making your own herb butters (*see Tip 410*).

299. Freezer fiends!

Freezing forms ice crystals, which may not be kind to some foods.

- Starchy vegetables such as potatoes will rupture their cell walls if frozen – the higher the starch content, the greater the loss of texture. So cooked or raw, keep potatoes out of the freezer as far as possible. (It doesn't matter in a soup, though, where a quick blend will sort things out; it will hurt a stew, however.)
- Crisp vegetables such as celery, onion, salad leaves, cucumber and even peppers will go limp!
- Whole raw eggs would crack in the freezer. As for cooked, the yolk should be fine but the white may go rubbery.
- Cheesecake suffers in the freezer unless artificially 'stabilized', so if it is homemade, you'd be best advised to eat it up.

■ Cold comforts

300. Stretch that date!

Open packages of even dry goods can
spoil gradually as they come into contact
with more and more air in a jar or canister,
especially if they contain oils that can go
rancid – breakfast cereals, for instance.

- If you doubt you can finish an open packet within
  a month of opening, put it in the refrigerator
  rather than a kitchen cabinet.

301. Don't decant dairy

When refrigerating non-solid dairy products
such as milk, cream or yogurt, it's best not
to decant them out of the original packaging
unless it's been damaged.

- These foods are especially sensitive to spoilage
  or tainting, yet are usually consumed uncooked.
  Changing containers increases the likelihood of
  contamination or exposure to both odours and
  microbes.

303. Fridge your own vinaigrette

Making your own salad dressing allows for endless customization – and it can keep at least a week as long as you aren't adding fresh herbs or garlic.

- The basic recipe is 1 tablespoon vinegar and 1 teaspoon mustard to every 3 tablespoons of olive oil (plus seasoning to taste, of course).
- You can vary it with spices and dried herbs – seeds such as fennel, cumin or coriander, chilli and garlic flakes, a little splash of balsamic vinegar, or some crushed dried herbs.
- The basic recipe can take an already-flavoured oil, vinegar or mustard for that extra punch.
- Refrigerate in a screw-top jar and shake well before use. This is the time to add in those fresh chopped herbs, garlic pods, or sun-dried tomatoes if you want.

302. Fish against freeze

You meant to cook the fish fillets and then didn't get round to it. And freezing will ruin the texture…

- Unless you're cooking at once, always place fresh fish on a layer of ice in a box and cover with more crushed ice.
- This way you won't have to thaw very long, yet it doesn't suffer the ignominy of 'freezer flaking'.

304. Dream creams

While leftover cream sits in the refrigerator, waiting to be used up, add one of these magic ingredients to transform it into a luxury sauce for desserts.

This works best with scalded cream – add the infusing ingredient as soon as possible.

- Add a spoonful of rum and a stick of cinnamon.
- Perhaps a spoon of bruised rose petals or dried lavender buds.
- For warm simplicity, a couple of lightly crushed cardamom pods.
- A couple of sprigs of rosemary and a spoonful of ground almonds.

305. Go yellow for keeps

Cooked rice is one of those foods that really isn't keen on sitting around in the fridge.

- If you're not sure you can use it all up, better add some turmeric to the cooking water and turn it yellow – that helps preserve the rice a bit longer, a lot better.
- This trick also works for vegetables and lentils, especially in soups (where the colour can be easiest to disguise if you have tomatoes, carrots or pumpkin giving it a dark reddish hue).

306. Ready to roll, again

Ready-roll icing dries out very fast – after all, it's meant to so that you can save time.

- If you've got some left over, wrap tightly in clingfilm and refrigerate in an air-tight box until you can use it up.
- Knead well before using, adding a few drops of lemon juice or glycerine to loosen if need be.

307. Glaze for the future

While not as stiff as fondant, royal icing or sugarpaste, hence not as prone to drying out, glaze-type or drizzle-on icings and whipped frostings have their own problems.

- Icing sugar glazes will quickly develop a skin on top that cracks while a moist pool develops below, trapping air and speeding up spoilage.
- Ganache icings tend to become gritty and lose their gloss if made to sit around.
- As for whipped frostings, they quickly deflate as the sugar picks up moisture from the air and weighs the fluffiness down.
- In all of these cases, put in an airtight container to refrigerate. But first, lightly press a layer of clingfilm on the surface to seal the freshness – and the texture – in.
- Try to use up within 2-3 days.

308. No loafing

One thing you really should avoid refrigerating is bread.

All too often, we think nothing of tossing the bag into the refrigerator to help it last another day. But for once, the humidity (that helps veggies stay fresh) will actually hasten mould in already yeasty loaves and buns!

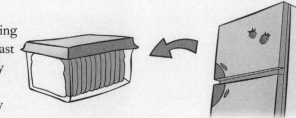

Store bread in a cool spot in an airtight box outside, or freeze outright.

■ From freezer to fire

309. You only heat twice!

That is to say, you can heat food to cook it and, after freezing, apply heat a second time to thaw – that's it!

- Never re-freeze food that has been thawed.
- When reheating food that was frozen and thawed, make sure it gets piping hot all through.
- If you mean to freeze it, do so as soon as possible – divide into small containers to cool fast and freeze at once rather than refrigerating, dilly-dallying, then freezing a couple of days later. Even if you don't end up with a mess of bacteria, the repeated temperature changes can ruin the texture of meats and vegetables alike.

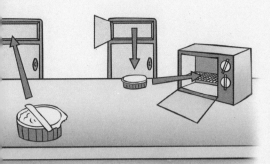

310. Hot from the freezer

Did you know hot baked soufflés can be made up to a day ahead and frozen?

- Prepare the soufflé mixture and freeze it directly in the ramekins you'll bake them in.
- Cover with freezer-safe clingfilm and freeze immediately to prevent the whipped egg whites collapsing. If your freezer has a quick-chill function, use that.
- When ready to bake, remove from the freezer and score a shallow cross on top to allow venting as it thaws.
- Pop straight in the oven and bake for an extra 5 minutes more than if baking fresh.

311. Go hot, go cold

Commercially available frozen vegetables and fruit retain better colour and texture because they have been pre-treated to optimize these properties.

You can certainly freeze your own fresh produce as well, but the results may not be quite the same.

- Fruits can tend to brown in the freezer, while vegetables lose their colour and go yellow.
- To prevent this, fruit needs to be acidulated – finding a freezing recipe for that particular fruit is your best bet (they tend to use ascorbic acid, but the amount varies).
- However, a little change in colour as well as the inevitable mushiness of texture shouldn't matter as much in a smoothie, pie or sauce.
- For vegetables, the best bet is to blanch them quickly before freezing.
- That means they won't need to cook as long later, which is why commercial frozen vegetables can be added to the pot straight from frozen.
- Without the blanching, veggies from the freezer will take a bit longer to cook – you'll have to account for thawing time to return the contents of the pan to the high temperature, as well as the usual cooking time of the raw veg.

312. Frozen fresh-bakes

Biscuits, like bread, respond rather nicely to freezing – for up to 6 months. But the dough lasts twice as long!

- So roll up a log and leave in the freezer.
- When you want some fresh-baked cookies, just slice off a few roundels with the bread knife and bake from frozen.
- If you pop them in just before dinner, they'll be ready to serve warm with coffee!

313. Slice and freeze!

Unlike biscuits – when you freeze, slice and bake – you need to follow the reverse order for bread.

- Slice up the baked loaf (it'll be a chore to cut up once frozen), then freeze the slices, interleaved with greaseproof paper.
- Later you can toast straight from frozen.

314. Cold coffee

Coffee beans stay at their best longer if they are frozen in an airtight container. You can grind directly from frozen.

- Scoop out just enough to grind for a single brewing each time, and brew right away – letting the beans or grounds 'thaw' at room temperature will attract moisture and encourage spoilage.

315. Frozen in shape

You have only so many containers, so you don't want them sitting in the freezer for months.

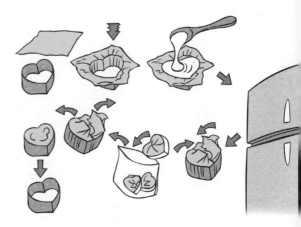

- If you make a terrine or pudding that will need to be baked in a specific mould, it simply can't be cooked or thawed in another container.
- So the cooking container must go into cold storage? No! Get the best of both worlds by lining the container in a double thickness of foil with enough excess around the edges to completely wrap over the top. Fill and freeze, then carefully fold up and close the foil package, and transfer the package to a freezer bag.
- Thawing time? Unwrap foil and slip the food, a block of the correct shape and size, into the destined container to cook or reheat. Neat!

Leftovers

Dinner-to-lunchbox 'recycling' suggestions; jazzer-uppers for plain-Jane staples; stretching sides to make a main; and sweet surprises from the remains of yesterday.

■ Starch turns sumptuous

316. Spaghetti snack

This is great for almost any kind of leftover pasta — just coordinate the vegetables with the sauce you started with.

• Sauté onions and sliced vegetables in a large frying pan.

• Stir the pasta into the pan.
• Beat and season several eggs – enough to cover the other ingredients – and pour over the mixture in the pan.
• When it sets at the bottom, add grated cheese and pop under a hot grill.
• Serve hot or cold.

It's worth making extra pasta just for this. If you start with double the quantity you need, you can also make this frittata with the leftovers.

317. Spiced rice

You should avoid refrigerating rice for more than a day – it spoils really quickly (*also see Tip 305*). However, it can be freshened up for your next meal with:

- Sautéed mushrooms
- Fried onions
- Toasted nuts and pumpkin seeds
- Grated or crumbled cheese
- Sweetcorn kernels and carrot julienne strips
- A can of drained beans or lentils with a pinch of cumin and a pinch of chilli
- Chopped fresh herbs, spring onions or shallots
- Currants, toasted coconut curls and turmeric

318. Stir-fried rice

Cold rice is actually better for stir-frying than freshly cooked because it won't turn mushy. The cold temperature of the refrigerator will have stiffened the outer layer of starch.

- Heat a little groundnut oil or sesame oil.
- Stir-fry some chopped bok choy and peeled prawns with a little crushed garlic. (You could also use spring onions, sweet peppers and sesame; or strips of meat, spinach and peanut butter)
- When the greens wilt, stir in a couple of spoonfuls of teriyaki sauce.
- Add the rice. Heat through and serve.

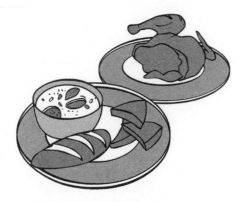

320. Keep the beans green

It's not a good idea to just refrigerate leftover steamed or blanched green beans as they will lose their crunch and colour.

- Refrigerate overnight, covered with ice water.
- Drain the beans and stir-fry with some garlic and tomatoes or lemon juice and zest.
- Add a little grated pecorino cheese or Parmesan cheese, or some toasted almonds.

319. Curried chowder

Almost any leftover meat or fish is fantastic in this milky chowder base.

- Sauté a couple of chopped onions.
- Add 2 cans of sweetcorn kernels.
- Stir in 300 ml/10 fl oz milk and 600 ml/1 pint stock.
- Season with dried herbs or curry powder.
- Simmer for 20 minutes.
- Meanwhile, chop up, shred or flake the meat or fish – about 225 g/8 oz is plenty.
- Use a hand blender to liquidize the soup.
- Stir in the meat or fish.
- Serve with Melba toast or some garlic bread made with a small sliced ciabatta or baguette.

321. Roasted root hot pots

With leftover roasted root vegetables, you don't need much more than some spices or herbs and either risotto rice or pasta.

- If you already added a good helping of herbs or spices to the roasting vegetables, don't add more.
- If you didn't, consider complementing the natural sweetness of root vegetables with pungent spices like coriander, cumin or chilli.
- Rosemary and sage go well with winter vegetables.
- Roasted onions make a great addition.
- Prepare a basic risotto with stock – no wine. Add the vegetables, diced, in the last 5 minutes of cooking. Serve with grated Parmesan cheese or pecorino cheese.
- Or cook pasta adding the vegetables. You could add toasted nuts as well – hazelnuts, chestnuts or walnuts. Stir in some blue cheese or soured cream to bind it all together.
- You can also add blue cheese salad dressing to the roasted vegetables with some crisp bacon bits.

322. Mediterranean vegetable mealmakers

Roasted summer vegetables – courgettes, aubergines, peppers and leeks – can be transformed into one-pot meals just like their winter counterparts (*see Tip 321*).

- For risotto, stir in the vegetables at the end. Add a spoonful of pesto or rouille for flavour.
- For pasta, mix in a vinaigrette made with strong mustard or a bit of pesto. For cold pasta salad, toss the vegetables with a balsamic dressing. Fresh herb garnishes could be mint or basil. If you'd like, add some baby mozzarella balls. Or supplement the vegetables with caramelized onions, grilled corn, or some stir-fried spinach.
- To make pizzettes, use toasted pitta bread for the base and layer the vegetables on tomato paste with cheese and pine kernels or sunflower seeds.
- For minestrone-style soup, bring a can of chopped tomatoes to the boil with an equal quantity of stock, adding some pasta and/or beans along with the vegetables in the last 7-10 minutes of cooking.

323. Cover up with cheese

A good store-brand cheese sauce can turn a batch of leftovers into a substantial bake. Some combinations from the day before:

- Strips of roast chicken, ham and leeks.
- Sautéed mushrooms and peas.
- Peas, asparagus, broccoli or spinach with ham or bacon.
- Sausage meat or meatballs with sage, onions and perhaps some chopped apples.
- Pineapple chunks and any meat.

- Refried beans and broccoli.
- Or, indeed, the classic cauliflower, given a twist by the inclusion of some orange segments.
- Throw in some cooked macaroni, and you have a meal-in-a-dish.

324. Curry-style sauce

The meat in a curry is usually demolished while the gravy lingers on. Don't throw it out quite yet!

- You can add chunks of fish and reheat for a quick new curry. Add a squeeze of lime and some coriander to finish.
- Stirring in a can of beans even before you refrigerate it will you give you a new dish. Check the seasoning after reheating, though.
- Or serve the curry base as a sauce with pasta, especially stuffed pasta.
- You can reheat the curry with some chopped green pepper and mushrooms to serve with rice.
- Or, simmer till it thickens and serve over grilled sausages or burgers.

- Consider simmering over a low heat with coconut milk or yogurt for a creamier sauce, and stirring in blanched green beans or baby carrots. Perfect as a soupy dish with egg noodles.
- A neat Indian trick is to halve and brown some hard-boiled eggs in a frying pan and add them to the curry.

325. Sangria fruit salad

Turn leftover sangria or rum punch into a dessert sauce for fresh fruit.

- Strain the sangria, reserving the fruit.
- Simmer the liquid with a pinch of allspice.
- Meanwhile, prepare fresh fruit to supplement the steeped pieces.
- When the sauce reaches the consistency of a thick syrup or coulis, pour over the fruit.
- Serve at once or chill until needed.

326. Pudding-ed ice cream!

Got some leftovers from a dense chocolate cake or plum pudding?

- Crumble it into plain vanilla, butterscotch or orange ice cream.
- You could add a shot of good brandy, single-malt whisky or schnapps.
- No need to break it up completely – a little bit of 'chunk' is fun! Scoop and serve as usual.

327. Rocky river

Here's a shake that no one will ever attach the label 'leftovers' to!

- If you ever have leftover cake, biscuits or brownies that have gone irredeemably dry, blend with ice cream and chilled milk.

Togetherness at the Table

Everything you need to know to bring mealtimes out of the nursery, without teething pains (though we have bite-sized solutions for that too). Age-wise edibles. Less-mess table-setting tricks. Menus for the whole family, from infant to old-timer – out of one dish!

■ Grown-up nursery meals

328. Small but sophisticated

Raise your child to feel at home with the tastes of a world full of choice and variety.

- Offer a meat-free meal from time to time.
- Offer more texture – use slices or small bits of meat instead of sandwich paste or frankfurters.
- Make the colours more intense – red cabbage instead of white; dark green leaves instead of iceberg lettuce; sweet potato rather than plain white potatoes.

- Add variety– a mixed mesclun salad rather than plain coleslaw; different pasta shapes instead of spaghetti.
- Let them try more exotic grains from time to time – couscous instead of pasta or bread.

329. Little grown-ups

While planning meals, treat your children as little grown-ups with some special needs – in the departments of chewing, handling cutlery and complicated finger food, and a few nutritional taboos. The early years are the best time to build good taste.

- Toddlers over the age of two are ready to eat in courses, just like grown-ups. If you and your partner are having a three-course meal, resist serving your child a one-dish mush!
- Making your child a sandwich? Ask yourself whether *you* would eat it. If not, don't give it to your child.
- Serve your child on a smaller plate with child-sized cutlery.
- Never serve your child adult-sized portions, even if it is a favourite dish.

330. Old favourites versus new friends

Children will have their favourites – perhaps your toddler prefers farfalle pasta to all other shapes; but make a game of having something 'new' every so often.

- You can have a 'new day' each week, when you try something your child has never had before, like an unusual fruit. Children like 'new'!
- And just so they know it's good to try something different although they have favourites, let them know you have favourites too! Say, '*My* favourite pasta is spaghetti, but today I'm making pasta twists because this sauce tastes nicer with it.'

331. Fledgling foodie (out and about)

The best way to encourage a child to experiment is to make the world of food into a big adventure.

- Children, no matter how little, will usually willingly try anything they helped 'pick'. Take children along for pick-your-own farm trips; at the supermarket, have them help you choose.
- Teach them how to shop – to look at simple labels (children old enough to add and subtract can assess price tags) and learn what differentiates a tasty fruit from a bland one.
- Always be up for adventure yourself – don't say no to samples unless you believe they are unhealthy and, if so, explain to your child why you said 'no'.
- When sampling at the farmers' market, offer your children a taste – suggest, don't insist, they try the 'stinky' goat's cheese; ask for their opinion and explain why something tastes the way it does.
- When they suggest an inappropriate purchase, explain why it's not a good idea and suggest a compromise.

332. Fledgling foodie (at home)

The food adventure (*see Tip 331*) should continue at home, and not just in the kitchen (*see Tip 333*).

- Avoid throwing out food – it's the worst example you can set because it signals that it's acceptable to waste food if you don't 'want' it.
- Shop sensibly, and plan meals based on what's fresh in the refrigerator and how many will be eating.
- Encourage your child to help you plan the menu. Leading questions should help even toddlers make an acceptable choice.
- Offer alternatives as suggestions, and explain why you think spaghetti with tomato sauce would be better than macaroni cheese.
- Consider growing a few easy vegetables at home – tomatoes are really easy – and 'help' your children tend them. If they grow it themselves, they will eat it with pride.

333. Fledgling foodie (in the kitchen)

Treat the kitchen as the fairground of culinary adventure. This is where all the action and excitement is!

- Even small children can 'cook' with a few precautions and careful supervision.
- Encourage children to have friends over for a make-your-own snack session.
- Let them have a hand in the foods they take to school – even if it's only stirring or throwing in the raisins. They'll glow with pride.
- They can top their own pies and crumbles and stamp out biscuits, as well as help you measure and mix.
- Allow them to experiment! It keeps them hooked, helps them learn and builds confidence. Older children can pick their own sandwich fillings or pizza toppings, for instance.
- If the experiment fails, be ready with words of consolation and encouragement – suggest what you might add or leave out next time.
- Most importantly, let them see you experiment – if you always cook only by the book, then they will soon come to regard cooking as the same as swotting from a textbook (which opens a whole new can of worms)!

334. Chubby cheeks

You don't want to encourage juvenile obesity by serving fat-laden food. But don't swing too far the other way either.

- Children up to the age of two need a larger percentage of food to body weight than adults because they can eat only much smaller volumes.
- Fat is calorie-dense and growing takes a lot of energy – the same calories would create a lot more bulk if they came from protein or carbohydrate!
- While this doesn't mean you need to add extra fat to food, don't remove it forcibly either.
- Never give your child low-fat versions of standard foods – so no skimmed or semi-skimmed milk yet and no 'diet desserts'.
- This is not a licence to gorge on fried food, however. Use healthier cooking methods most of the time.
- Shift towards the same lower fat guidelines as for adults when your child starts school.

335. Kiddie carbs

A baby's transition from low-carb milk feeds to complete fibre-rich adult food must be gradual.

- Introduce the first carbs (apart from baby rice) at nine months.
- At this point, you don't want to give too much fibre. So begin with bread, porridge, potatoes, rice or pasta first.
- After a couple of weeks you can start adding puréed root vegetables and blander fruits such as apples or pears.
- Beyond age two, toddlers should be able to digest most carbohydrates, including high-fibre vegetables and fruits, quite comfortably. But not too much of those – they still need their lower-fibre grains. And no high-fibre grains until they're five!
- By the time they approach school-going age, you can start the transition to an adult type diet in terms of the fibre balance.

336. Drink up

A baby's tiny stomach is easily filled by liquids. Too much fluid will prevent the absorption of essential nutrients.

- Avoid offering a drink with a meal until the child is at least two.
- Offer a drink after the meal, though.
- In very hot weather, offer a small sip up to half an hour before meals.
- For toddlers over the age of two, offer a small cup of water, milk or well-diluted unsweetened fruit juice.

337. Safely sterile

It's not just your baby's bottle, bowl and spoon that need sterilizing.

- Also scald any utensils used for food preparation– knife, chopping board, sieve, blender jar and saucepan – in boiling water.
- Placing everything together in a deep roasting tin or stock pot and pouring in boiling water from a kettle is the quickest, least messy way.
- Keep a set of separate utensils for your baby's food, making sure the chopping board and saucepan are smaller in size.

338. Baby batches

Blending your own baby food (*see Tip 357*)? Save time and avoid waste by making several batches at once.

- A baby will typically eat only a small amount of the purée you offer – from a teaspoon early on to 55 g/2 oz while still supplemented by a milk feed.
- That's why a sterilized ice tray produces the perfect portion sizes.
- Freeze and then pop out the cubes to secure in freezer bags or a lidded container. Label clearly.
- Don't keep for more than three months. You should actually use it up much faster because your baby will outgrow the smoother textures quite quickly!

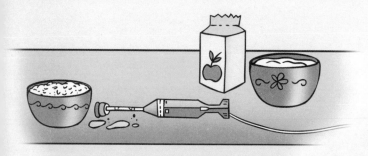

339. First foods

Some ideas for those first purées.

- Don't hesitate to blend more than one vegetable with formula milk. Which ones go together? That's the same as for adults.
- Be careful about adding fruit to milk, as it might curdle. Thin with puréed apple, baby rice or apple juice.
- You can also add a little 'grown-up rice' to a purée.
- When the baby is six months old, you can start leaving the purée a little chunkier, perhaps even process the food to a fine mince rather than blend to a purée. Occasionally you might add a little carefully deboned chicken or white fish.
- Now you can also start introducing stronger flavours – a little red meat, tomatoes, mushrooms, mild hard cheese and a little onion.
- That's when you can start adding tiny pinches of herbs and spices, maybe even a hint of garlic, too.

340. Egg-citement

It's certainly a very nutritious and tasty food, but little babies can't digest egg very well.

- Don't give eggs to babies under six months.
- You should only give them hard-boiled yolks, not the whites, between six and 12 months.
- By 12 months, however, a baby should be quite comfortable with whole eggs.

341. Purée inspiration

Think about your own favourite foods when inventing purée combinations. These combinations are suitable for babies over six months.

- Fruits with custard powder and milk will be very well received.
- Try yogurt with banana or any combination of fruits you might serve in a smoothie or sundae (peach Melba!).
- How about a mix of Mediterranean vegetables?
- Or try a kedgeree-style rice purée – add a little white fish, some peas and a little hard-boiled egg yolk to rice and milk.
- Rice with a few carrots, cauliflower, potatoes and peas is very satisfying.
- Be adventurous with fruit purée mixed with some chicken.
- For purées that include meat, consider replicating the ingredients of a classic stew or casserole.

342. After nine months

By nine months, a baby's teeth are starting to appear, so progress to chunkier food.

- Baby food need no longer be a purée; move to a rough mash or finely chopped meal.
- During teething, babies will appreciate finger foods to gnaw – offer peeled fruit, raw carrots or cucumber sticks, and small pieces of chicken, ham or fish. Not too much ham, though, as it is very high in salt.
- Your child might not mind a little more seasoning at this stage – such as the flavour of stock.

343. I can do it myself!

As soon as your baby starts making a grab for the spoon, you should start providing pint-sized cutlery.

- At first, a bowl and spoon to play with will be enough – you can go on with the real job of spooning in without fear of too many grabs.
- While still giving fine purées, put a little in the bowl for the baby to play with.
- Don't worry if the baby digs in with hands rather than spoon! Just make sure the little hands are clean.
- Once teeth appear, some finger food while you feed – cooked carrot, broccoli or cauliflower at first, then bits of bread or toast – is a good idea.
- Finally, allow the baby to attempt to feed himself or herself – and don't intervene when he or she makes a mess! It's the only way to learn how.
- Put newspaper under the chair as well as the tabletop! Carry some with you when visiting with your baby.

344. Join the table!

When your baby's just starting to feed himself or herself, you will get a chance to concentrate on your own meal for a few minutes.

- This is when the baby can start sitting at the table, at a high chair pulled up.
- Offer chopped or minced food for eating with a spoon. This should be about half the meal and your help and attention will be needed.
- The second course can be finger foods – bread-based, vegetables or toast.
- This gives you a chance to finish your own meal and start tidying up.
- It also establishes the habit of eating in courses!

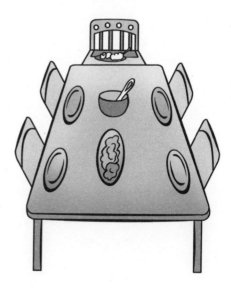

345. First snacks

A baby about to turn one is a natural snacker! After all, young children expend a lot of energy playing and growing, so it's not reasonable to expect three small meals in tiny tummies to last all day.

- Offer simple finger foods at first (*see Tip 342*) and let the baby take his or her time. He or she will stop automatically once full.
- Avoid sugary snacks because once that taste for sugar is acquired, it is very difficult to get a baby to eat a savoury or blander food!
- Now that a little more salt is tolerated, cubes of mild hard cheese, pieces of French toast, chicken nuggets or fish fingers are of interest.
- Gradually move on to offering mini sandwiches or bread with a mild sandwich spread to get the baby used to 'real' food.
- Popcorn and cheese straws are usually popular.
- Don't give whole nuts to under-fives (*also see Tip 346*)!
- Stick mainly to fruits and vegetables, and occasionally dried fruit.

346. Now I am one

Most foods will have been introduced by now and some of the rules can be relaxed.

- Reserve miniature fairy cakes or shortbread as occasional treats.
- It's time for real breakfast cereals, and even sausages!
- Ground nuts can be given to babies over 12 months, but monitor carefully for any adverse reaction.
- Avoid the pudding-after-every-meal habit, otherwise the child will soon learn to avoid or eat less of the main course!
- By now definite likes and dislikes are taking shape, so be wary of snacks – too many will ruin the appetite for meals.

■ Nutrition in the playschool

347. Good for you

As your child develops preferences and gets more active in and outside home, keep an eye on the nutritional content of snacks.

- Snacks of raw vegetables and cheese to end a meal combat tooth decay, which frequent snacking and sugary foods can encourage.
- Children should drink full-fat milk to get the benefits of fat-soluble vitamins. If there's great resistance to plain, offer a flavoured drink (but check just how sweet it tastes and keep it light). Also check with your doctor that there's no lactose intolerance.
- From time to time, reintroduce the 'hated' foods in new forms. Growing children make up their minds afresh all the time!
- Many foods that have previously been spat out will be tried happily if offered as part of an 'experience'. The adventure might be a picnic, a 'camping trip' (in a tent in the garden) or a toys' tea party.

348. Smarter sandwich

Just because all the kids at playschool have sandwiches with mayonnaise doesn't mean you must offer your toddler the same!

- Instead of sad, squishy white bread, rotate different traditional breads for sandwiches. Try pumpernickel, Irish soda bread, seed and multigrain breads, foccacia with tomatoes.
- Or turn the sandwich into a pitta pocket or tortilla wrap.
- Look beyond mayonnaise to pesto, hummus, grainy mustard, mild pâtés, even a good quality ketchup that's not too sweet or synthetic.
- Think of a pizza as an open sandwich – easy on the cheese, more veggies and a wholewheat crust.
- A vegetarian sandwich needn't be cheese by default. Use roasted peppers (very good with hummus), spinach with mushrooms or sweetcorn with sprouts.
- Few children will turn down peanut butter and banana. Make it an occasional treat.

349. A lunchbox to love

Children are attracted to a wide variety of textures and colours, since they are biologically programmed to be inquisitive enough to learn! And that need not mean smiley faces on everything – not all your child's heroes are clowns, are they?

- Make it interesting to look at and hold as well as taste. Broccoli 'trees' bordering a 'field' of sprouts sown in a bed of potatoes…
- Keep up the novelty value. Vary the juice box, yogurt and fruit.
- Keep them 'growing'. Don't just opt for the simplest option (banana or grapes) each time – try a new fruit. Such as physalis or cape gooseberries.

350. Kids' kebabs

Many children will turn up their noses at chunks of vegetables on a plate, but will gladly pop them in if those same chunks are threaded on a skewer!

- Start easy – alternating chunks of salmon and cod for a fish-finger addict or just presenting cocktail sausages on a stick.
- From there, go on to a mix of the familiar and the different – ham and pineapple with cheese, sweetcorn with sausage slices, peppers with fish.
- Once they are happy with that, add one of these – chunks of courgette, cubes of baked pumpkin or sweet potatoes, button mushrooms, cherry tomatoes.
- You can even make fruit kebabs – bananas to begin with (serve a chocolate custard to dip in) and then gradually grapes, melons (balls for the pale ones or dice for watermelons), wedges of peaches or plums, kiwi slices and star fruit.

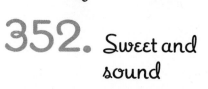

351. Hide and treat

If the appearance of a new food threatens to put your toddler (or slightly older child) off, adding a favourite to it should induce them to give it a chance.

- Pair fish florentine with dinosaur pasta shapes.
- Serve a wild mushroom sauce on toast with a grilled cheese slice.
- Falafel 'veggie burgers' should quickly banish a reluctance to eat chickpeas.

352. Sweet and sound

Dessert needn't be a nutritional disaster.

- Make frozen yogurt lollies.
- Serve fruit dippers with chocolate custard.
- Instead of bought ice cream (often too sweet and fatty), make fresh fruit sorbets or stir fruit purée into custard to freeze for 'scoops'.

353. Fussy eaters

Some ways to deal with a fussy eater:

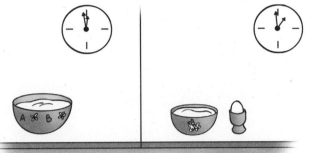

- Reduce portion sizes.
- Don't make a fuss – if he or she is just playing with the food rather than eating, quietly remove the plate.
- See if it is possible for a favourite adult or a small friend to be present at some meals. Don't draw attention to the child's eating habits.
- Offer new foods when the child is really hungry.

354. Mama's little helper

Get toddlers to play their part in the mealtime ritual early. That sense of participation – rather than being forced to sit quietly (which seems like punishment) – can make a world of difference.

- Ask them to lay the table for you.
- Encourage them to pass the condiments. Expect a mess of salt, pepper and butter initially!
- Setting a place for teddy can be a great incentive.
- Switch to shatterproof dishes for a bit!

■ Everybody eats

355. One-stop meals

You can introduce small amounts of meat, chicken, white fish and yogurt to babies over ten months, so even with a toddler and a baby in the family, plus any older children, careful planning will allow you to cook just one basic meal.

- Of course it will have to be 'finished' differently for various age groups.
- Keep things bland as late into the cooking process as possible – this way, making baby's purée is just a matter of chopping, blending and straining.
- While it cools, you can season the rest – lightly for the toddler.
- Set that out and let it cool too while you add grown-up ingredients to the rest of the portions – the alcohol reduction, the chillies and heavier doses of garlic, sautéed onions, the soy sauce, the curry paste, the whole eggs, the nuts.
- Always check the temperature of children's food before serving.

356. Eating together

Make it a habit to eat together at the table as a family whenever possible – that means no one is excused unless they are not home or there is a genuine crisis.

- Baby joins the table in the high chair and will make a grab every so often – avoid a tablecloth under hot dishes, and keep knives and teapots out of reach!
- Toddlers will sometimes start to fuss over what you choose or demand to eat in front of the TV. Explain that your family eats together. If baby resists, serve food at the table and otherwise ignore him or her. Steel yourself to stay calm in the face of a tantrum. If it gets too distressing, sit the child down in a different room.
- Older family members must set an example by never getting up until everyone has finished eating.
- If the child changes his or her mind and decides to eat at the table, have the whole family sit down again till he or she is finished – this serves as encouragement and reinforces the point that you eat *together*.

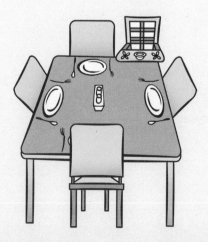

357. Baby blender

A smaller-sized blender jar is one of the best investments you can make for a baby starting on solids.

- You can easily turn any fruit, vegetable, cooked cereal and even a portion of whatever you are eating into baby food that's far nicer than any can or jar you may buy.
- Cut up small portions of everything and blend, adding a little water, milk or apple juice if necessary for a smoother texture.
- Strain to remove fibrous bits, pips and stray fish bones.
- If offering a portion of what you are eating, season your food later.

A baby fed on blended adult food tends to move to 'proper' food more readily!

358. Toned down for tots

Toddlers above the age of two can start eating meals quite similar to your own. However:

- Avoid anything very spicy. Certainly no chilli peppers or hot sauce yet, and keep the pepper down.
- Remember that a concentration of herbs or spices that is perfect for you may be too much for a tiny tummy.
- Tone down the onions and garlic. You can sauté some and add to your own food separately later.
- Season the adult portions at the table – salt should be avoided in a child's diet.
- Anything that contains alcohol or a high concentration of caffeine is out. Even with chocolate, avoid high cocoa percentages.
- Avoid adding too much sugar.

359. *All-family smoothies*

It's worth buying a blender just for these!

- Whether made with yogurt or milk, smoothies provide a quick, delicious calcium boost laced with fibre and potassium.
- They can serve as breakfast, a side (instead of milkshake) or a snack.
- They're quick to slurp when in a hurry and easy to drink on the go.
- They're endlessly versatile – besides fruit, you can add seeds and nuts as well as some grains (toasted oats, cornflakes).
- They're a whiz to make, and anyone over 12 should be able to make one safely and successfully; even under-tens might do well with some supervision.

360. *Mediterranean mini menu*

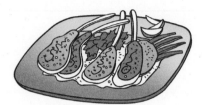

If you're serving lamb chops and roasted Mediterranean vegetables:

- Simply skip the seasoning on one of the chops.
- Process half the unseasoned chop with some vegetables for the baby.
- Slice the other half for a toddler to eat with vegetables and some toast.

362. Curry for kids

Craving a curry?

- Hold the coconut milk and curry paste until you have cooked the meat or vegetables and have reserved the children's portion.
- For a toddler, you can mix in a little yogurt and serve the 'curry' on a bed of rice or pasta with a piece of naan bread.

361. Hot pot-lets

Making lamb hotpot?

- Prepare the filling and set aside the children's portions in a separate casserole.
- Add some rustic sausages to the remainder, or a little Guinness if you prefer.
- Top both casseroles with potatoes and bake according to the recipe directions.
- Serve with boiled Brussels sprouts.

364. Tex-Mex tots

Does chilli con carne sound unsuitable for small children?

- Hold the spices and seasoning, and cook the mince with more vegetables than is strictly traditional – mushrooms, peppers, peas.
- Don't add any beans yet – the skin of the red kidney bean is tough on immature tummies.
- Put the children's portion of cooked mince in a casserole dish and bake with a few small scrubbed potatoes alongside.
- Season your own chilli with spices, stir in the beans and simmer until cooked.
- Spoon the toddler's portion into halved and hollowed-out potato boats.
- Adults will get a green salad and soured cream on the side, and can melt some cheese on the potato skins under the grill!

363. All Greek to us!

Moussaka is easy to manage for a family!

- Cook the mince with a very light seasoning.
- Spoon the toddler's portion into a ramekin.
- Season the adult portion to taste with garlic, salt and extra herbs or spices.
- Top your portion and the toddler's with potato slices, putting less cheese and more breadcrumbs on the ramekin than on your own.
- Leave to cool for a bit after baking. (You can reheat yours, if necessary.)

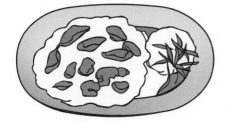

365. *Very Continental!*

Yes, you can even adapt beef bourguignon to a tot's tastes!

- Hold back the wine, garlic and bouquet garni.
- Brown the meat in a saucepan and simmer in some stock and tomato purée with a small sprinkle of dried herbs or the corner of a bay leaf.
- Spoon the children's portion into a separate casserole dish.
- Simmer the adult portion with the wine and adult-only seasonings.
- Bake both sets until meltingly tender, adding shallots and mushrooms to the adult portion.
- Serve with shredded steamed cabbage and mashed potatoes.

366. *Starting to stir-fry*

Children tend to be fascinated by the matchstick shapes of colourful vegetables in a stir-fry.

- Brown a few pieces of pork or chicken in a saucepan.
- In the same pan, stir-fry vegetable matchsticks without soy sauce and garlic, throwing in some mung bean sprouts.
- You can use stock and cornflour, perhaps even a little ketchup.
- Set aside the stir-fry and, for the adults, toast some cashews and fry a little garlic with soy sauce. Toss into your portion.
- Serve the toddler portion in a Chinese bowl, perhaps with a 'Chinese spoon' for atmosphere (a soup spoon works here because the pieces are small enough to spoon up, but don't be surprised if the matchsticks are treated as finger food!)

367. Casseroles on a roll

Even with little children, casseroles remain the most fuss-free one-pot meals for friends and family.

- Seasoned lightly, most casseroles can be puréed directly into baby food, adding whatever vegetables you would have served on the side (as long as they are well cooked).
- For toddlers, you need to cut up only the larger pieces. They should be fine with the standard side dishes – a little salad, some peas, broccoli, carrots and new potatoes.
- If you think it might be too bland for adults, make a little roux and stir in extra spices and perhaps a fruit relish to serve on the side.

368. Too tiny for turmeric

Cooking curry from scratch rather than with a readymade paste or powder?

- Toddlers over 12 months should be fine with turmeric as long as you use a light hand.

369. Tandoori tonight

Introduce your toddler to ethnic tastes early with this crowd-pleaser. It's close enough to grilled chicken that most children take to it readily.

- Marinate chicken pieces in yogurt mixed with a pinch of turmeric, a little sweet paprika and some mixed herbs.
- For older family members, add curry paste and chilli to the marinade after reserving the children's portion.
- Grill until the juices run clear.
- Serve with cherry tomatoes, cucumber sticks, onion rings (just a couple soaked in cold water for finger food) and some naan or pitta bread. Add a spinach salad for adults.

370. Salad stuffers

There may well come a time when you are desperate for a lighter meal of salad. But you still need to cook something more nutritious (i.e. calorie-dense) for the children, right? Not necessarily.

- If you're making Caesar salad, salade Niçoise or cold chicken salad, simply use the meat or fish as the basis of your children's.
- To make it more substantial, serve the children's portions in toast cups – bread squares pressed into the cups of a muffin pan to toast so it has a hollowed shape perfect for filling.
- You can open a can of sweetcorn or add some chopped sweet peppers to the children's portion, while keeping the olives to yourself.
- Mix in some mayonnaise and yogurt for the children to make a creamy scoop.
- Add a little of the creamy dressing to your own along with lots of crisp salad vegetables and leaves.
- Decide whether to serve them the hardboiled eggs based on their age (*see Tip 340*).

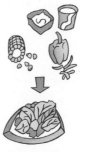

371. Fish foods

Traditional dishes such as paella and kedgeree are great for special occasion meals at home with young children. Their colourful mixed-up appearance holds great charm.

- Stick to plain white fish for small children – no in-shell shellfish or cured products yet.
- Toddlers are old enough to eat a small peeled prawn, however.
- You can add squid rings, mussels, prawns or smoked fish to yours separately, cooked with turmeric and saffron.
- Even fish cakes can be a complete meal with the addition of some grated carrots and chopped greens.

372. Vol-au-vous?

Small individual vol-au-vents are easy for children to pick up and eat.

- Make them more attractive still by using animal shapes (*see Tip 377*).
- Fill with fish or hard-boiled eggs and vegetables in white sauce, creamed corn and peppers, with a sliced pimiento-stuffed olive, to garnish.

373. Versatile vegetables

Consider serving meatless meals now and then to give vegetables a starring role.

- Grilled cheese on toast is a great start – add vegetable toppings as though making pizza. You can lay on tomatoes, roast peppers, mushrooms and sweetcorn to begin with. Wait a little to introduce courgette and aubergine slices.
- Tomato-based pasta sauce is another great base – you can chop or grate in just about any vegetable with good results.
- Slightly older children will enjoy a vegetable crumble with beans, with a cheesy, seed-speckled topping, in individual ramekins.
- Try bean burgers or falafel in pitta pockets, drizzled with tahini.
- An onion tart may be too much for children, but they'll probably love a tart of leeks in cheese sauce.

374. Sweet stop

Don't make puddings a daily habit. Keep them for weekend treats. Some easy ideas:

- Bread and butter pudding is a nursery favourite!
- Eve's pudding usually goes down well too.
- For a teething tot, baby carrots 'glazed' with jam and rolled in coconut shreds is fun. Older children can use honey for 'glue' instead.
- Everyone likes peaches or strawberries with cream – and shortcake! No strawberries for babies under 12 months, though!
- Fruit brulées are healthier than caramel custard.
- Make individual apple turnovers: place the filling at one end of a strip of filo pastry and fold over the corner, continuing to fold to make a triangular 'pie'.
- Pavlovas are easy to mess with and eat!
- Whole baked apples and poached pears appeal to most children. Tarts are family favourites, but tartlets are easier for toddlers to eat.
- Make mousse by whipping cream, fromage frais (or yogurt) and jelly. Swirl through puréed fruits.
- A parfait of fruits in jelly alternated with a set mousse in a sundae glass will appeal to children.
- Most children like fruit salad – and it's even easier when it's a dried fruit compôte. Or add bananas and oranges to dates and raisins for a warm fruit salad.

■ Big plates, small plates

375. Toddler trays and small plates

By the time they are off to playschool, hand-eye coordination will have improved.

- For toddlers, cut up larger pieces of meat or vegetables into bite-sized chunks or slices.
- A slightly older child will be happy to feel grown-up when you serve him or her the same way you serve yourself (chicken leg with bone in; whole fish steak).
- However, be prepared to help with the cutting up if the going gets tough.

376. Portion control

Children might eat the same foods as you, but certainly not in the same quantities.

- To help a child's plate look more like your own, choose a smaller (salad) plate in the same design. That way, the smaller portions will be perfectly in proportion.
- For 'portioned' foods such as meatballs or hamburgers, thaw and reshape to make smaller patties.
- With foods that won't allow you to do that, halve the portions – 2 fish fingers to your 4; 1 scoop of yogurt to your 2; a single small wedge of pizza, and so on.
- With some foods, you can simply choose a smaller size for the child – a junior-sized baked potato or a smaller whole fish.
- In other cases, just serve half – this works well with most fruits and other symmetrical foods.
- However, half a muffin is less appealing than a miniature. Ditto a burger or pie.

377. Shapely servings

Let the look be lighthearted – under-fives are unlikely to be ecstatic about nouvelle plating! They may well prefer a broccoli 'forest' with pomegranate 'fruit'!

- Make fish cakes in a fish shape – use a biscuit cutter or mould by hand.
- Or support a fishy dish with vegetable slices cut like fins.
- Pepper and carrot 'stars' brighten up most dishes. You can even pillow them on potato clouds or hang them off a broccoli Christmas tree!
- Make baked potato boats with cheese or ham sails.
- However, don't clown around with every meal. Sometimes a bright-rimmed plate provides enough fun to offset a delicious dish.

378. Beef up the bread!

Sometimes, the 'same old' boring slice needs to be brightened up.

- Cut out a toast moon and stars and tuck into scrambled egg clouds.
- Use gingerbread cutters to make bread people and let the child use sandwich toppings of his or her choice to dress the food 'family'.
- Make striped cheese toast by alternating strips of white mozzarella, yellow Cheddar and Red Leicester.
- Or play noughts and crosses in a grid of vegetable strips with ketchup counters.
- How about a clockface pizza? Use biscuit cutters to punch the numbers out from coloured peppers, carrot or cheese slices. Add ham hands!
- If you have a steady hand, spell them a pancake message.

Easy Entertaining

Quantities to feed a few or a frenzy; last-minute, super-quick and no-cook ideas; sure-fire recipes for larger groups; conversation-starting afters; serving suggestions for special diets; and economical entertaining options.

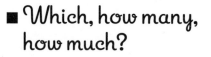

■ Which, how many, how much?

379. How many for dinner?

Don't overestimate the number of people you can comfortably seat or cater for.

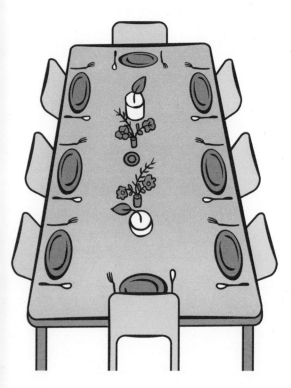

- For a sit-down dinner, 6–8 people is a comfortable number.
- You can go up to 10 or 12 provided they are family or close friends, willing to pitch in with serving and clearing, or if you have hired help.
- Any more and you should consider a buffet or barbecue instead.

380. Enlist some help!

Whether you're serving a sit-down hot meal, a cold buffet or cocktails and finger food, you can't cook, serve and clear up all by yourself.

- Ask someone else to set the table while you cook, or to top up drinks while you bring out the munchies.
- For a sit-down meal, delegate clearing up and bringing out fresh dishes – if one person has to do both, guests will be waiting a long time between courses!

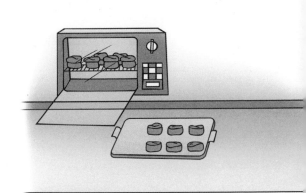

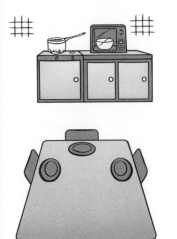

381. A big business

A buffet usually implies a longer guest list. Simplify your prep:

- Should friends offer to do something, accept and suggest they bring bread, dips or relishes, cheese, biscuits or salad.
- Roasts, terrines and mince-based pies or curries remove some of the headache of portioning while still looking elegant and eye-catching.
- Avoid steaming hot or frozen cold dishes, especially for dessert – there's no way you can serve 10–12 people at a consistent temperature and it's unfair to make those first served wait until the last serving has been dished out!

382. At the bar

Six people jammed together at the home bar. Too much pressure on the 'bartender'. If you have a larger number of guests, consider setting up more than one bar area.

- For parties of over 12, have two bar stations.
- If the party is in the garden or on the terrace, diagonally opposite corners are a good bet.
- If you open up more than one room, a single bar will mean traffic snarls! Put a bar station in each room.

383. Red or white?

Serving wine? How many different types should you buy?

- If it's just wine and nibbles, stop at two or three. Choose red, white and either a rosé or a sparkling wine (or a sparkling rosé!).
- Alternatively, offer two whites and a red.
- If you're serving a variety of drinks at a summer party, you could skip the red – fewer people will opt for it.
- What to serve with meat if not red? Ask at the wine shop. Some of the bolder New World whites partner gamey flavours well.

384. Hot or cold?

Don't try to cook fresh or reheat everything to piping hot for more than 10–12 guests.

- If you're doing a buffet, offer hot and cold dishes in equal proportions.
- Or have just one or two (one vegetarian) freshly cooked dishes with cold accompaniments.
- Or go for a cold fork buffet.
- You can serve a hot dessert following a cold buffet, although, on a hot day, people will probably be glad to have something cold.
- For canapés, alternate cold and hot. (Send out the first two nibbles almost simultaneously; then appear with each subsequent one at twenty-minute intervals.)

385. How much each?

A rough guide of dinner party portions for a typical adult:

- Main course fish or meat, bone-in cuts or steaks – about 225 g/8 oz.
- Fish or meat as starters, or cut into boneless goujons, or served as pâté or terrine – about 85–115 g/3–4 oz.
- Rice or pasta – 1 cup
- Bread – 2 large slices or 2 small rolls
- Salad – 150 g/5½ oz
- Vegetables – 150 g/5½ oz
- Dips, dressings and sauces – 2–3 teaspoons each
- Fruit or pudding – ½ cup, 1 medium whole fruit (small apple, medium peach or large kiwi) or mini muffin-sized portions of individual puddings.
- Drinks through the evening (pre-dinner and with meals) – 2–3 glasses wine or cocktails, 3–4 whiskeys or glasses of punch, 3–5 shots of spirits or liqueur, plus mixers.

386. Dinner and drinks

If you're serving drinks before dinner:

- Don't offer more than 3–4 types of nibbles. A single crowd-pleaser is fine if dinner will have a few courses.
- Serving just one snack? Keep it vegetarian, and free of common allergens (avoid nuts!).
- Allow about an hour before serving dinner, but never delay more than 2 hours from the start of the party.

387. Noodles for all the neighbours

Adapting pasta recipes is easy.

- Allow 75 g/2¾ oz dried pasta (125 g/4½ oz fresh) per person.
- If you're cooking for a big crowd, test whether the pasta is al dente several minutes *before* the recommended cooking time – and stop when close. A big batch of pasta keeps cooking for a bit, even after draining, because heat is held in.

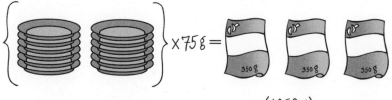

388. Gobstoppers!

Or 'What Not to Serve' to prevent conversation-halting bad breath! For an even remotely formal lunch or where in-laws, clients or colleagues are involved, *avoid*:

- Pickled onions
- Radish
- Sauerkraut
- Garlicky dips (roasted garlic – *see Tip 267* – is fine, though)
- Hardboiled eggs (except a little as a garnish)
- Stinky tofu or dried prawns (and most other fermented foods and dried fish or seafood)
- Highly scented tropical fruits such as Hawaiian noni and Southeast Asian durian; even pawpaw can be a bit much for some.

If you must serve these, pass around some strong mints after the meal!

389. No-ice impasse

If you are preparing ahead for a large dinner party, you will need your freezer to be as empty as possible for the make-ahead dishes, so you may not have room for ice trays!

- Hire a small freezer, make the ice well ahead and bag it up for transfer, or borrow a neighbour's freezer space!
- Alternatively, buy ice cubes on the day.

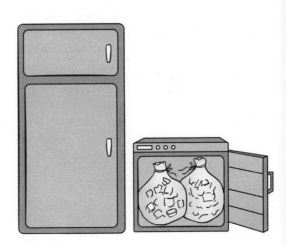

390. Picnic packs

Having a picnic? Bring along a couple of hand towels to supplement serviettes.

- They are handier for mopping up.
- You can moisten them with water to clean sticky fingers.
- They're much more eco-friendly than wet wipes.
- On the other hand, baby wipes are better against stains!

391. Al fresco extras

You've got the food and drinks, but you should also have:

- A large bin liner for disposing of debris
- A bottle of soda water in case of spills (to wash out stains)
- A first-aid kit
- Insect repellent
- Sunscreen
- A large plastic sheet – to sit on if the ground is damp and as protection in case of a sudden shower.

■ The bar's a breeze!

392. Cocktail by the carafe

Unless a professional bartender is present, it's best to dispense with a long drinks list for large parties.

- Serve no more than three kinds of liquor – red, white and sparkling wine; beer, rum and coke; or just a single flavoured vodka.
- Or serve one stellar seasonal drink – sangria or punch in summer, mulled wine or egg nog in winter.
- Provide a non-alcoholic alternative.
- If you're hell-bent on having a signature cocktail, stick to that (plus its teetotaller version).
- When choosing a party cocktail, it's better to opt for a blended rather than a layered drink. You can keep it ready mixed in a jug, then pour and decorate fast.

393. Quick-chill champagne

Haven't time to put your whites and sparkling wines in the refrigerator before company arrives?

- Put the bottles in a plastic bag and tie off before plunging into an ice chest or a bucket of iced water for 10 minutes.

This protects the label and keeps the bottle dry for a non-slip grip as you pop the cork!

394. Flat bubbly?

As you pour out the champagne, half the glasses instantly lose their fizz! The rest are fine. What's wrong?

- If you washed them in the dishwasher, traces of detergent may have attached themselves to your flutes – that's what killed the bubbles!
- Rinse glasses well by hand and wipe dry with a clean tea towel to avoid this.

395. Punch with no punch

For underage guests and designated drivers amongst your guests, make up a non-alcoholic fruit punch.

- Spike a 1-litre / 1¾-pint jug of ginger ale with the juice of 4 lemons, a couple of oranges, a couple of grapefruit and a can of pineapple. Serve chilled, with an ice ring (set in a ring cake tin or aspic mould).

■ Nifty nibbles

396. Swift sticky sausages

It's the humble sausage to the rescue for trouble-free entertaining:

- Roll cocktail-sized sausages in Thai sweet chilli sauce and grill until well browned. Make lots – about 6–8 each per guest – and don't bother about other bites for an hour-long party!
- For a longer do, wrap very thinly-sliced bread around each sausage after grilling to add substance!

397. Under wraps

These clever cocktail snacks are easily wrapped up:

- Strips of Parma ham around breadsticks (grissini) or asparagus.
- Spicy salami slices around a sweet bite – prunes, perhaps?
- Cheese wrapped in bacon slices and zapped in a medium oven for 5 minutes.

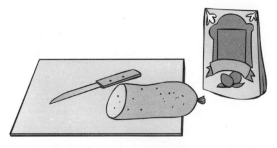

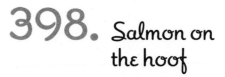

398. Salmon on the hoof

Smoked salmon is a lovely starter for a sit-down meal – with just a dollop of crème fraîche, a grind of pepper, some dill and a few capers. This can be translated into a manageable snack for serving with drinks.

- Roll slices of salmon around a dollop of peppered cream cheese with mustard.
- Pop a caper inside.

399. Cheesy cucumber boats

These cheese and chutney canoes make a refreshing and unusual bite!

- Get thin-skinned baby cucumbers, bite-sized, if possible.
- Split lengthways and hollow out in the middle.
- Add a few cubes of diced cheese and a fruit preserve or jelly. Quince goes with most cheese; try a hot mango chutney with a blue cheese.

401. Enoki in obi

An easy and impressive snack that's halfway between sushi and a bacon roll!

- Warm some strips of bacon in the microwave oven.
- Wrap a small bundle of enoki mushrooms in each bacon strip.
- Cut the bundles in two, splitting the bacon strips.
- You now have one set of enoki heads with a bacon ribbon around the end, and another slimline bacon roll 'stuffed' with the ends of the mushrooms.
- Serve with wasabi mayonnaise or a honey-mustard dip.

400. Not pineapple with cheese on sticks

Sticks of cheese with pineapple too retro? Try a twist on an old theme.

- Start with a mature hard cheese.
- Make up on cocktail sticks with quartered fresh figs, diced mangoes, dried apricots or prunes.
- Add a dribble of honey or sweet chilli sauce.

403. 'You're the life of the party'

Got a mixed group of friends not mutually acquainted over for coffee?

- Pass around a box of fortune cookies to liven things up and break the ice.

402. Help party animals 'jell'

Pass around an 'adult' version of jelly shots for a barbecue or poolside do.

- Dissolve jelly crystals in a solution of 2 parts water and 1 part vodka, white wine or white rum.
- Use small ramekins or tumblers to set individual portions.
- When partly set, add some grapes, berries or sliced fruit – kiwi, starfruit or kumquats; avoid pineapple as it interferes with setting.
- Leave them a little jiggly for bar-style shots.

404. On the side

Choose side dishes for ease and speed.

- Mix together a green salad to go with a hearty main course such as roast vegetables or a casserole. If it's summer, crisp leaves dressed with vinaigrette is sufficient. For winter, try bacon lardons or slices of salami with wilted spinach; for vegetarians, exchange the meat for bits of onion and roasted almonds.
- With fish, sausages, burgers or a ham, consider a side of mixed roasted vegetables (*see Tip 269*) so you won't have to do potatoes, rice or pasta separately.
- Need a lighter vegetable? Try leeks, fennel or escarole in chicken stock and cream gratinéed with Parmesan cheese and breadcrumbs.
- Crisp greens such as Brussels sprouts, broccoli or green beans can be quickly blanched to seal the colour, then warmed through before serving with fried garlic slices, pancetta or toasted nuts and a pinch of cumin seeds.
- When you have a rich meaty main course, consider serving a fruit compôte or pan-fried apples or pears instead of a dish of vegetables plus gravy or cream sauces.

405. Posh jackets

Yes, you can tart up the humble jacket potato!

- Halve the potatoes – they'll cook faster too.
- Cut a cross in the flesh of the cut side and bake skin side down.
- Scoop out some of the centre and mash it with your filling. Pile it all back in.
- Update the fillings too. Instead of tuna salad, try salmon or smoked haddock. Instead of baked beans, use Puy lentils and celery. Substitute grilled Mediterranean vegetables for coleslaw.
- Drizzle with a few classy condiments – salsa with sweetcorn, capers and soured cream with the fish, pesto on the vegetables…

406. Peas or potatoes?

You might think you're adding a 'vegetable' when you serve a dish of peas along with the potatoes. Blame it on their colour!

- Peas – like beans – are high enough in carbohydrates to substitute for the potatoes!
- Choose another vegetable instead.
- Serve either peas *or* potatoes as the carb-rich staple.
- If you can't give up either with the traditional Sunday roast, pass on the bread basket.

407. Layered fans

Make a basic dish of baked Mediterranean vegetables special by interleaving the vegetables in a 'fan'.

- Line the base of your baking tin with sliced onions and crushed garlic seasoned with crushed coriander and herbes de Provence.
- Slice aubergines or a large plump courgette lengthways, with the stem end left intact, so that they resemble folded Japanese fans.
- Tuck slices of tomatoes or strips of red pepper between the 'blades' and lay on the bed of onions.
- Fill any gaps with bay leaves and mushrooms, olives, fennel, artichoke or other succulent vegetables.
- Add another layer of onions and garlic before drizzling with olive oil.
- Cover and bake at 190°C/375°F/Gas Mark 5 until the vegetables are tender.

408. Hot and hearty

This fantastic vegetable dish looks impressive and doesn't demand much from the cook.

- Dice any winter vegetables to hand – potatoes, sweet potatoes, pumpkin, carrots, parsnips – into 1-cm/½-inch pieces.
- Add diced onions and whole cloves of garlic.
- A couple of red peppers or a bunch of tomatoes will add a succulent texture as well as colour, but don't worry if you don't have any.
- Pile into a large roasting tin and mix in a handful of rosemary, salt, a little balsamic vinegar and olive oil.
- Bake for about 30 minutes at 190°C/375°F/ Gas Mark 5.
- Stir in a can of beans or chickpeas and bake another 20 minutes.
- To make this a posh vegetarian alternative to the standard roast main course, add a grating of good Parmesan cheese or pecorino cheese, mixed with 2 spoonfuls of soured cream, at the end.
- For vegans, top with toasted pine kernels and other seeds instead of cheese.

409. Full head

This makes a lovely vegetable-rich centrepiece for a special dinner.

- Remove any blemished outer leaves from a whole head of cabbage and trim the stem so it 'sits' stable.
- Simmer the whole head in salted water for 10–15 minutes, or until the outer leaves have become supple enough to bend without breaking off.
- When cool enough to handle, place on a large piece of muslin before pulling back the outer leaves to expose the heart.
- Cut out the heart and finely chop. Sauté with cooked rice, bits of ham and peas, seasoning to taste.
- Press this mixture back into the cabbage and fold the outer leaves back into place.
- Bard the cabbage with bacon strips and tie up the muslin.
- Bake in the oven till a skewer passes readily through the toughest area, at the base.
- Lift into a bowl or pudding basin, untie the muslin, place a soup plate over it and upend to transfer to the plate.

410. Better butter

Whether for topping a barbecued steak or garnishing the mashed potatoes, herb butter looks deceptively posh. It's hardly any trouble at all, though.

- Just whiz about 2 bunches of fresh herbs – chives, parsley, coriander or mint – with 75 g/ 2¾ oz butter in a food processor for a couple of minutes. When you see the herbs floating around in bits, it's ready.
- Now place pats of it in the middle of rectangles of greaseproof paper or freezer-safe foil.
- Roll up sausage fashion, twisting the ends like a bonbon to seal.
- Chill until needed – or freeze several rolls for long-term use.
- Slice or dice into a cold dish to serve.

411. Stars for your steak, posies for your toast

No butter stamper to personalize your pats?

- Use little petit four cookie cutters or clean play dough stamps to shape and chill butter on a flat tray or baking sheet. Tumble into a chilled dish just before serving. A galaxy with your bread basket – impressive!

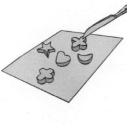

412. A drizzle to garnish

Weight-watchers and those avoiding saturated fats won't be too pleased with the flavoured butters (*see Tip 410*). Try this fresher, more modern take on garnish-with-extra-flavour.

- Mix powdered spices or chopped herbs (you can thaw the ones from *Tip 298*) into a good extra virgin olive oil – cumin and chilli make a lovely pep-up, as do mint or coriander leaves.
- Drizzle over pasta, cooked fish or chicken, even float a little on soups or smear on croûtons. It's nice on pizzas too.
- Consider a hint of fruity olive oil over puddings and fruit salad instead of a thick creamy sauce or custard. Flavour with scraped vanilla pods, a pinch of cinnamon or some lemon zest (*see Tip 162*).

413. Bitter sweets

Decoration for fresh fruit and desserts needn't always be fruity or sweet! Sharp spices and herbs can be an unexpectedly deep counterpoint.

- Sprinkle chilli powder on chocolate mousse.
- Serve melons or citrus fruit with a grinding of fresh pepper.
- Dredge churros and waffles with paprika and sugar rather than cinnamon-sugar!
- Offer celery salt with intensely sweet fruits such as mango or pawpaw.
- Consider a little roasted and powdered cumin on poached or stewed fruits.

414. Sweeten for savour

A judicious hint of sweetness can uplift savoury classics to fresh heights.

- Scatter lavender instead of mint on roasting lamb.
- Tuck dried rose buds under the skin of a roasting chicken and baste with honey and yogurt.
- Add half a teaspoon of ground cinnamon and/or a grating of nutmeg to lentil soups.
- Pumpkin pie spice is good in creamy winter soups too, even cauliflower!
- Add a spoonful of sugar to pumpkin risotto.
- Extra sugar enhances the natural sweetness of carrots and peas.
- Honey, like chutney, is good with anything involving cheese!
- Add melon chunks and strawberries to summer salads.
- A few squares of plain chocolate can do wonders for a root-vegetable casserole as well as for spicy meat curries.
- Mix some aniseed paste with the potatoes!
- Complement coconut milk in curries with raisins.
- Marmalade is fantastic on fish!

415. Drip-free lollies

Ice lollies are easy favourites. But they do get messy as they melt…

- Push the stick through a foil muffin cup, paper doily or coffee filter to catch the drips!

416. Three pretty meringues

Ready-made meringues double as coffee companions and dessert starters – always have some on hand. For a quick sweet treat:

- Sandwich meringues together with a filling of 2 parts whipped cream and 1 part each of mascarpone cheese and lemon curd.
- Roll sideways in flaked almonds so they stick to the filling.
- Serve with some juicy soft fruit – berries or mangoes, or perhaps a few chocolate-dipped cherries.
- Chill liqueur-laced cream in individual cocktail glasses and float a meringue on top.
- Cave in the peak of individual meringues with a quick, light knock from the wrong end of a spoon.
- Add a teaspoon of chopped fresh fruit in the hollows.
- Pipe a swirl of sweetened whipped cream on top and drizzle some puréed berries (fresh or frozen), strained persimmons or crushed pineapple bits on top.

417. Supermarket special!

When you've no time for a homemade pudding and store-bought will look too tacky, buy:

- A rich chocolate loaf cake
- 250 ml/9 fl oz double cream
- A jar of dulce du leche or toffee sauce
- A can of sweetened chestnut purée
- A small bottle of coffee or chocolate liqueur or syrup
- Split the cake into 3 layers and sprinkle each with a tablespoon of liqueur.
- Whisk the cream to get soft peaks.
- Mix together the can of chestnut purée, 125 ml/4 fl oz dulce du leche and a spoon of liqueur.
- Fold in the cream.
- Sandwich the cake layers with this mixture and top with some grated chocolate or chocolate flakes.

Pipe a pattern in toffee sauce on top – or just drizzle over. Serve in thin slices.

418. Panettone perfection

A high-domed loaf of panettone makes an impressive sculptural gâteau.

- Slice the panettone into three horizontal layers.
- Spread the bottom and middle layers with some whipped mascarpone cheese flavoured with fruit liqueur or grated plain chocolate.
- Add chopped fruit and sandwich together.
- Sprinkle icing sugar and decorate with a sprig of herbs (mint or rosemary go beautifully) or a few edible flowers (nasturtiums, roses or violets).

Voilà! A stunning centrepiece that you can eat after dinner!

419. It's a snip

The quickest cake covering ever, whatever the shape.

- Cover the top and sides with whipped cream – don't bother smoothing.
- Press chocolate curls along the edges to make a ruffled trim. (You can make the curls by pulling a swivel-bladed peeler along the smooth back of a chocolate bar at room temperature.)
- Fill the centre with a pile of fresh berries and serve.

420. Lighten up the fruitcake

Unless it's Christmas, a dense fruitcake covered in fondant icing is too much.

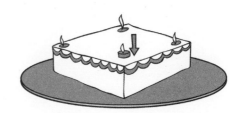

- Lighten up on the icing or forgo it altogether.
- Decorate by pressing in blanched almonds – you can write a message with the nuts, or pattern a swirly design instead.
- Or wreath it in light alone. For candles, try tea lights set in little tins. An appropriate number on the cake's surface will double up as decoration.
- Big-number birthday? An age cake is perfect for more mature years. Pass up the candle-blowing, and stick in the appropriate number of sparklers instead!

421. Candle savers

Dripping wax from the birthday candles can mess up those sugar roses. Save the day by using little props for your candles.

- Slices of marshmallow, Turkish delight or liquorice allsorts make good taper stands, if you're happy to sacrifice some.
- So do ring-shaped sweets.
- You can also make little foil flowers to collect the drips – cut out 4-cm / 1½-inch flower shapes; place on the cake and press candles into the centres. When done, lift off the candles, let the wax congeal, then peel away the foil and discard.

423. Fruitier toppers

Whether you're serving a ready-made cake or want a quick dress-up for your homemade one, some ideas:

- Use a potato peeler to take the peel off a large orange or lemon in one continuous strip. Loop the curls in a clump on a honey-glazed tea loaf.
- Cut the thinnest slices you can from the centres of whole apples and whole pears, peel and stem still in place. The cross-sections should be vertically down (along the core) for pears and horizontally through the apples. Lay alternate slices, overlapped, along the rim of a cake. Drizzle with melted preserves or ice cream topping.
- Cut slim wedges from unpeeled pears or pineapple rings. Cut inch-deep slits on the surface of an un-iced cake. Push the wedges in carefully so that the narrow end sticks up sail fashion.

422. Stained-glass shards

Here's an artistic garnish for puddings or ice cream.

- Line a baking sheet with foil and grease.
- Line up several identical, metal, greased biscuit cutters on the tray.
- Drop 2–3 small boiled sweets into each cutter.
- Put them in a low oven for about 5 minutes, or until the sweets melt into puddles.
- Leave to cool and peel off foil.
- You can use a tart tin with a removable base for a large sheet. Break into shards to stick upright into a sundae or soufflé – at the last minute or it'll melt away!
- Or use assorted colours melted together to make a 'tabletop' cake topper, piping royal icing around the circumference to anchor in place.
- Consider decorative shapes too, using metal biscuit cutters as moulds.

424. Sugarcrust surprise

Here's a cheat to making that lovely crunch on top of a crème brûlée.

- Lay a sheet of foil on a baking sheet and brush oil on it in ramekin-sized circles.
- Sprinkle an even layer of brown sugar inside the circle – don't worry, it doesn't have to be very regular in shape.
- Place under a hot grill for 2–3 minutes or until caramelized.
- Leave to cool before peeling up carefully.
- Top a custard pudding in a ramekin – just before serving, or the disc might melt!

425. Citrus fluff

This refreshing dessert makes a cloud-light impression on your guests.

- Loosen some good quality lemon curd with passion fruit pulp.
- Mix together equal parts sweetened whipped cream and Greek-style yogurt.
- Layer the two in a shot glass, add some toasted shredded coconut on top, and serve at once.

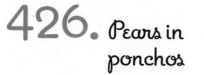

426. Pears in ponchos

For something stunningly posh yet effortless, wrap peeled and cored pears (stem on) in puff pastry.

- Cut small squares of puff pastry for the pears to sit on.
- Glaze with some jam and place on a lightly greased baking sheet, then sit the pears on them. You can even add a chopped chocolate, cream cheese or chestnut purée core.
- Roll out as many larger squares – the length of the sides should be about the height of the pears.
- Cut a little diamond out of the centre of each and slip over the stem of each pear to drape like a poncho.
- With a sharp pastry knife or scissors, snip the edges for a tasselled 'fringe'.
- Bake till the pastry crisps up.

427. Custard with crunch

Make a plain custard tart special by adding your own secret topping!

- Line the rim with a ring of dried apple or pineapple slices.
- Or use crystallized flowers – violets, pansies or rose petals brushed with egg white and pressed gently into fine sugar.
- Or scatter with little lozenge shapes cut out of angelica or citrus peel.
- How about a simple scattering of orangettes – those chocolate-covered strips of tangerine peel?
- Elegant enough for a party: a line of after dinner chocolate mints, each topped by a maraschino cherry.

428. Tart transfer

Individual tartlets are chic and easy – but can be messy to cart around if the filling is oozy or crumbly. So what to do when friends request your signature mushroom tart for their barbecue?

Turn them into pielets!

- Start with double the amount of pastry specified in the recipe.
- Instead of tart cases, use baking sheets.
- Pretend you're going to make mini calzones – cut out rounds of dough, fill and fold into crescents.
- Or cut squares to fold into 'fingers'.
- Otherwise, sandwich the filling between two circles. Brush the edges with water and crimp the edges with a fork to seal.
- Or stamp out the dough with biscuit cutters in an apt shape – from gingerbread people for a reunion to a cottage to welcome a new neighbour, to stars for a summer dance…

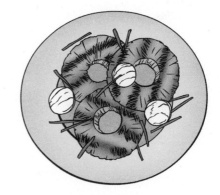

429. Cheese course… or fruit?

Why not both? Serve a two-in-one dessert/savoury course of fruit with cheese, plus a herb or spice. Try:

- Juicy pears with a Stilton and walnut ball filling in for the core.
- Cubed watermelon topped with crumbled feta cheese and fresh mint.
- Sliced apple and Cheddar cheese, with a sprinkling of cinnamon sugar and raisins.
- Fresh figs stuffed with goat's cheese and thyme or lavender honey.
- Pulped mangoes with a grinding of pepper and Parmesan tuiles.
- Grilled pineapple garnished with preserved ginger slices and dolloped with ricotta cheese.
- Lychees hiding a small blob of chilli- and cumin-marinated mozzarella cheese balls in the centre.

430. Pizza finish

Stun your guests by following a grilled main course with a pizza!

- Top the pizza with torn up pieces of a ripe Brie or Camembert and halved green and red grapes.
- Brush with olive oil and bake.
- Serve with a glaze of melted bitter marmalade.
- Alternatively, try Roquefort or Stilton with pears and walnuts, garnished with rosemary dipped in honey.
- Or shredded Gruyère, Cheddar cheese or provolone with prosciutto and figs, served with port.

431. Lite-est libations

Anyone watching their weight? Offer a choice of lower-calorie drinks that won't starve their sweet tooth.

- For those happy to drink alcohol, but looking for a healthier mixer than cola or canned juices, offer one of the many fruit-flavoured waters now available.
- As a non-alcoholic alternative to champagne, try a flavoured sparkling water.

432. Gluten-free canapés

A finger-food base other than the predictable rice cakes if your guest is allergic to gluten?

- 5-cm/2-inch chunks of cucumber from which a hollow has been scooped out with a melon baller.
- A thin 1-cm/½-inch slice of cucumber or courgette is a good alternative to toast.
- Crisp endive leaves.
- Asparagus spears, celery sticks or roasted spears of parsnip.

Make sure you dry the vegetables well before assembling and serve soon, lest they go limp.

433. Meat-free menaces!

Anyone on a red meat-free diet for medical reasons? When providing a meatless menu for them, be careful that you don't add a lot of dairy instead – although cheese may seem to be a logical swap, it's full of saturated fat.

- Substitute with lean meat or nuts, or simply with lots of vegetables and beans.
- Or see if using a low-fat cheese or yogurt will allow you to tweak a meat recipe.

434. Sugar-free sweetness

For those avoiding sugar for health reasons, offer a sweet beverage free of synthetic chemical additives.

- Brew coffee and tea with a small cinnamon stick or a vanilla pod, or offer one as a stirrer – most people find they don't miss the sugar with these added 'dessert' flavourings.
- A crushed cardamom pod or a grating of nutmeg can have the same effect.
- Sometimes, spice can reduce the need for sweetness! Chilli with cinnamon in hot cocoa, a pinch of pepper on fresh fruit, or a little fresh ginger in tea...
- Use fruit purées to sweeten puddings (apple sauce can also substitute for fats in many cakes and baked confectionery).
- Instead of fizzy drinks, offer water (plain or sparkling) with just a splash of natural fruit juice.
- Instead of flavoured, pre-sweetened fruit yogurts, offer natural Greek-style yogurt with honey and fresh fruit on the side that guests can help themselves to.

435. Spare the salt cellar

For those on a low-sodium diet, stock up on:

- Low-sodium salt, as long as it's approved by your doctor.
- Highly flavoured herbs and pungent spices – including garlic, turmeric, chilli or paprika, pepper, ginger, oregano, parsley, coriander, tamarind.
- Lime juice.
- Sodium-reduced or salt-free meat stocks.

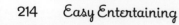

■ All about afters

436. Coffee companions

There's nothing wrong with offering a basic chocolate treat with an after-dinner espresso.

- Make a tiny extra effort, though – remove the wrappers and perch one on each saucer rather than passing the box around.
- Slip in a cinnamon stick for stirring the coffee.

Now that's elegant.

437. Water-free chocolate

Why not serve a cup of luxury hot chocolate instead of pudding, then coffee?

- Melt together 200 g/7 oz dark chocolate in 250 ml/9 fl oz cream in the microwave oven , at just under full power.
- Add a spoonful of the chocolate cream to each cup and top up with steaming milk.
- Sprinkle with cinnamon or coffee, or have a shaker of vanilla sugar to hand.
- Offer shortbread or strawberries with this.

438. Hot milk spiced up

Another decadent after-dinner drink. This one's a great liquid lullaby for guests who will be staying overnight. It's also the perfect palate soother after a spicy meal.

- Heat 1 litre/1¾ pints milk with a couple of cinnamon sticks, and 3–4 (each) cloves and cardamom pods.
- Leave to stand for a couple of minutes to infuse, discard the spices (*see Tip 192*) and serve.
- Decorate with flaked pistachio nuts and stem ginger, or sprinkle just 2–3 strands of saffron on each frothing cup.
- Ginger nuts are perfect with this.

439. Dinner in a dash

Unannounced dinner guests? No time to shop?

- Some pasta or potatoes, or even a more exotic grain like couscous or basmati rice, is easy to cook on the side.
- The fastest dinner-plate anchor is a piece of grilled meat or fish.
- For vegetarians who are happy to eat eggs, an omelette is the perfect option.
- For strict vegans, consider a stew of canned lentils or beans and quick-cooking vegetables simmered in coconut milk and curry paste.
- Steam some green vegetables or mix up a green salad or easy salsa of chopped tomatoes, chillies, coriander and peppers.
- Garnish the meat or fish with a special homemade sauce – *see Tip 440*.
- For dessert, crumble some biscuits or cake into vanilla ice cream, or drop scoops of ice cream into espresso for an indulgent *affogato*.

440. Salsa-fy!

A dish of boiled macaroni, a slice of bought pizza or hamburger patty can all be 'fancified' with a really good sauce.

- Make your own pesto – food processors, mortar and pestle or even chopping ingredients finely by hand will do. You'll want 55 g/2 oz nuts to every 2 handfuls of herbs and a good olive oil to loosen, plus a proper Parmesan cheese to grate over.
- Roasted peppers and/or tomatoes, peeled and mashed with garlic, perhaps a chilli and a couple of herbs are even easier to throw together.
- If you've got a tropical fruit or some avocado, chop it up and mix with some sliced red onions or chillies, some cucumbers and either lemon juice or crème fraiche for a quick salsa. You can even purée this and serve as a dip.
- Jazz up some plain butter by folding in chopped capers or green peppercorns in brine, a little sharp English mustard, and a few sprigs of any fresh herb you've got.
- Chopped fruit, fresh or canned, can be simmered with any pan juices and a splash of wine to make a fruity relish.

441. Cheese first?

Super-short on time? Bring the cheese course up front and skip the soup!

- Pare down the courses to nibbles, one main dish and a pudding.
- Cook just the main course yourself – roasted balsamic vegetables (*see Tip 269*) mixed with beans or grilled farm-style sausages is just fine.
- For the rest, buy good quality basics that won't need dressing up.
- Get a good artisan cheese and a couple of different kinds of bread – one fancy (such as foccacia or similar), one plain (ciabatta or baguette).
- Serve the plainer bread with cheese and wine by way of a starter.
- If you still think it needs bolstering, a cheese such as feta or mozzarella can be marinated in warm olive oil with a few herbs, spices and flavourings (chilli, fennel, garlic, shredded basil and citrus peel are just some options).
- Serve some olives (you can marinate them like the cheese, but warm through together with the oil) and roasted nuts sprinkled with chilli pepper.
- Serve the flavoured bread with your main course.
- For simple, satisfying pudding ideas, *see Tip 442.*

442. Pudding? Done!

- For a summer dessert, opt for peaches (or another soft fruit, such as mango) and ice cream, with a bit of toffee or fruit sauce, or a sprinkling of pistachio nuts.
- In winter, serve pan-fried fruits. You can sprinkle over some wine or liqueur, or serve with custard if you have some.
- Don't ignore the possibility of biscuits for a grown-up sweet! Instead of milk, though, serve with citrus curd and fudge or chocolate ganache (melt chocolate and whip in cream).
- A compôte of fruits garnished with toasted coconut or edible flowers may be all you need.
- Or just serve berries with cream.
- A crumble is quick to make, bakes while you sit down to dinner (*see Tip 274*), and is hugely satisfying.

■ *Off-peak party hours!*

443. Affordable entertaining

Rather than counting the costs of every dish when you're entertaining on a budget, look to adjust the basic plan.

- When resources are limited, veer away from dinner or elaborate luncheons.
- Alcohol is a money-guzzler. If a toast to the occasion seems a must, restrict it to a cocktail evening rather than doing dinner *and* drinks. With a mid-grade champagne or a sparkling wine or prosecco you wouldn't need other options.
- Revive the old-fashioned afternoon tea. Keep it light – don't turn it into high tea!
- For close friends, family or business associates, meet for breakfast.
- Get together with friends for coffee after a night at the theatre or an art show – chances are they will have eaten before or nibbled during. Serve a few pastries, a sweet wine, brandy or liqueur, and of course coffee, tea and a choice of biscuits.
- For a smaller number, a picnic is always fun.

444. Breakfast fruit for a queen

Pawpaws aren't just good, they're great – chockful of vitamins and other antioxidants, fragrant and sweet, plus easy to prepare. And filling enough for a breakfast 'main'. Add a zingy syrup for special-occasion garnish.

- Boil up some syrup with lime juice and zest. Add a sprinkling of orange flower water or rosewater.
- Drizzle over pawpaw slices, add a grind of pepper and garnish with some edible flowers – white or blue look stunning on their sunset hue.

445. Chill-out picnic

You start out with chilled drinks and cold food, but by the time you sit down to it, the food's at room temperature. On a hot summer's day, this is an invitation for bacteria to thrive.

- If you're packing any liquids, freeze them in small watertight containers.
- Distribute these throughout your hamper to keep other foods cold, making sure everything is in water-resistant packaging (so they don't get soggy as the frozen foods 'sweat').
- Alternatively, put a Thermos flask of ice cubes in the middle and pack food around it.
- Bunches of grapes that start out frozen will be just nicely chilled for lunchtime.
- Oh, and carry that hamper with you in the car – it's too hot in the boot!

446. Sushi tonight?

To minimize your prep, why not get together for sushi?

- Put together individual bento boxes from your local sushi bar. Let that be the star of the menu.
- For appetizers, avoid tempura; try steamed edamame or spiced nuts (*or see Tip 401*).

- Offer miso soup on the side – made from a mix, garnished with chopped spring onions and tofu.
- Cold soba noodles tossed with toasted sesame seeds, light soy sauce and honey will satisfy anyone still hungry.
- For afters, serve fresh fruit, tea or sorbet.

Setting the Table

A place for every family member and guest, appropriate to every meal – from casual family dinners to formal luncheons; conversation-stopping table décor: centrepieces, flowers and candles given a fresh slant too

■ *Lively linens!*

447. Cute cutters!

Taking a little trouble over the table linen will add a sense of occasion.

- Roll up serviettes and thread through biscuit cutters.
- Add savoury biscuits in the same shape to the cheeseboard or serve sweet ones as petits fours.
- Give each guest a little bagful. Dangle one out of the bag on ribbon – pipe on the guest's name; they double up as gift tag and place card!

449. Old lace updates

Put crochet doilies and vintage lace to a new use.

- Sandwich a doily between dinner plate and charger or the decorative underplate.
- Add pearl or jet beads to weight the 'rim' and use atop carafes and jugs.
- Link them into a long chain or a floral round – no need to match – for a special table dressing.

448. Soft landing

Thick tablemats will prevent china scratching the table and add tactile pleasure.

- Make your own with plain felt rectangles.
- Paper punches can make a patterned perforated border. Pinch up folds at random points near the margins and punch through with the punch, just edging out beyond the crease to get two interlocked shapes out!

These are particularly handy if you like to stack plates and bowls together at each place setting.

■ A place (setting) for everything

450. To match or mis-match?

When in doubt, resort to bone white – use plain chunky china or stoneware every day. Classic and stylish shapes are good for entertaining too. If you don't have enough of the same type of crockery, resort to a mix. To make it look considered rather than cobbled-together include:

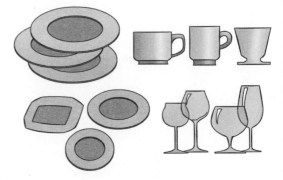

- Several colours in the same shape or several shapes in exactly the same hue.
- Mix no more than two or three shapes and colours for plates, bowls, glasses and cutlery.
- For wine glasses, coffee and teacups, you can go for a wider variety – in which case, each piece can be different! Tell your guests it's to help them remember their glasses.

451. Tots' table

With tots just learning to eat, a mess is inevitable.

- To protect your best table linen, supply sheets of Sunday comics.
- If you can't do without a tablecloth, choose chocolate brown (hides most stains while suggesting cocoa!)
- Or, use plain white (which will withstand the toughest bleaches).

452. Your glass, or mine?

ID-ing your glass can be quite a challenge at a cocktail do.

- For an informal evening, borrow your daughter's hair bobbles. Make sure they're all different, then slip one onto the stem of each glass.
- For a more formal do, use glass beads on a twist of wire.

453. Buffet in order

Most people put the cutlery at the front, alongside the plates and napkins – and the polished silverware slides about on fine china, getting in the way of food.

- Start with plates and napkins.
- Then offer the main dishes – salads and sides; accompaniments such as bread or pasta or rice come later.
- Put the condiments at the end.
- Have the forks, knives and spoons last.
- Let guests know that the sweet course will be served separately – on a different table or sideboard, or in individual portions along with coffee.
- The cheeseboard should sit on the sweet table.
- Soup gets a table to itself (clear it away and put the pudding there later). Set the bowls out first, then the soup tureen, then spoons.

454. Shakers to the centre

Where does one place the salt, pepper, pickles and relishes?

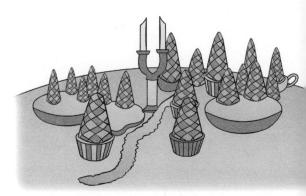

- For an informal get-together, have just a small set on the sideboard, in the centre on the table or near the hostess. Pass around as needed.
- For anything less casual, the condiments should be clustered in the centre of the table for a party of up to 10. Any more, and you'll need two of everything near the ends of the table.
- Put all the condiments together in a small basket if there are more than two.
- If serving sauces and gravies in boats, dot them around the table, between and close to the main dishes they support.

455. A forest of fir (cones)

For an almost imperishable, yet always remarkable table decoration:

- Fill small tealight holders, larger candlesticks, ramekins and dip bowls with sand.
- Try to choose a single type of material – white china, silvery metal or even foil muffin cups.
- Sit a fir cone in each and line up the container 'forest' in an undulating row down the table.
- You could add a track of gravel or sand beneath to pull it together.

456. Eggs-otic centrepiece?

Asking friends over for brunch? It may be too early to nip down to the flower shop.

- Why not pile some fresh eggs into a wide, squat vase or pretty bowl instead?
- Or put them in an old fashioned basket.
- Don't pile them too deep (prevents messy cracks).
- If you think that looks sparse, add a few fresh herbs or baby vegetables. Or mix brown and speckled shells!
- Baby carrots make a nice counterpoint to the eggs in terms of colour and shape; broccoli florets are sweet too.
- Or have a separate basket or two of mushrooms and/or whole nuts – just make sure you're cooking the mushrooms the same day.
- Or just use some well-washed twigs from the garden.

457. Garden fresh, from the market

Sometimes you want to make a really special impression:

- Scrub some plain terracotta flowerpots and sterilize.
- Dab an appetizing home fragrance or diluted essential oil – apricot, orange, cinnamon, herbs, lavender, vanilla, almond…
- Pile some fruits and nuts into the container with a few spices and herbs that coordinate. Select just one kind or a theme that includes no more than 3–4 ingredients. Your theme may be colour-based or inspired by a favourite dish, or even seasonal – green apples and bay leaves with a few blueberries; peaches and apricots with cinnamon; oranges stuck with cloves.
- Line them along the centre of a long table. Or cluster together in the centre at different heights – stand one on an upturned saucer, another on a small upturned pot, and so on.

458. Frosted fruit

Pressed for time?

- A bowl or platter of mixed fruits can make a fine centrepiece. Add a dusting of icing sugar to make it look special.
- Or you could just tuck in bundles of cinnamon (tie together with kitchen twine or ribbon), some star anise, the odd pine or fir cone, maybe acorns and nuts.
- If you do have a few moments, a bowl of like fruits – pears, say – can be given an identical dab of edible gold or silver leaf each. Brush the spot with egg white, lay on foil to stick!

459. Seating plan, all lit up

For a simple casserole or roast, with a fruit or ice cream dessert, prepare a special table setting – with oranges:

- Use the tip of a vegetable peeler to scrape the peel away in thin curly strips, letting the white show, to 'etch' your guests' initials. Or simply poke in cloves to print their nicknames!
- Sit them in small ramekins (to prevent them rolling over!) and stick a candle in each to have it serve as candleholder. Let the guests light their own. The warm wax will bring out the aroma from the peel. Neat!

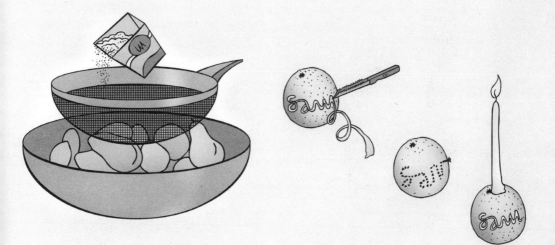

■ Flames and flowers

460. Peppers burning bright

A delicious bit of table décor combines plain tea lights with vegetables.

- Cut the tops off peppers and slip in the tea lights.
- Sit them in small saucers or dip dishes for safety.
- Line up the peppers – all one colour or a regular series.
- Or cluster them together to make a many-petalled flickering flower.

461. Canned flowers!

Use empty food cans for this delightful arrangement.

- Cut vegetable sticks, preferably green, to match the height of the can – unpeeled cucumber, celery, leek leaves, chard stems, stalks of courgette flowers or even the woody ends of asparagus.
- Slip a rubber band around the tin and start tucking in the vegetable sticks until the tin is covered.
- Tie with florists' twine or raffia and remove the rubber band (left on, it might crush the 'stems' as it tightens).
- Fill the tin with water and arrange the flowers.
- Place on a saucer with a splash of water to 'feed' the stalks.
- Colourful flowers look best with green; but if you chose white or blue flowers, a shot of rhubarb red, pepper yellow or carroty orange might yield riveting results.

462. ...Or bottled blooms?

A variant of the idea in *Tip 461* that lets you use fewer flowers over a larger area.

- Select narrow-necked bottles of roughly similar proportions.
- As in *Tip 461*, line the outside of the bottle with slender stems –wild garlic, woody stems of herbs such as thyme or rosemary.
- Secure them to the tapering shape of the bottle with two ties, near the base and beneath the neck.
- Add water and a single delicate flower in each.

463. Teacup full of posies

Another lovely arrangement to complement a summer garden party.

- Use co-ordinating sets of teacups and saucers as 'vases'.
- Nestle some florists' foam into the base of each cup.
- Add flowers and foliage in a tight burst.
- Put a teaspoon on each saucer with a sugar cube on it, or just balance a fragrant teabag against the cup.

Party Planner

Themed ideas for invitations, menu ideas and serving suggestions, occasional dishes, party favours and/or small gifts, and even a cake to match!

■ Organized entertaining

464. Party prep

Good planning means your party will go with a swing!

- Send invites a fortnight to four weeks ahead, depending on numbers and formality.
- State the date, time, venue and dress code.
- Set an RSVP date and provide both email address and telephone number.
- Finish major repairs or cleaning jobs before you tackle food and decorations.
- Check if linen and dishes are clean and cutlery is ship-shape.
- Use place cards to stick to a seating plan.
- For a buffet, dance or cocktail event, figure out the traffic paths and organize furniture accordingly.
- Keep the music ready.

466. Teens? Be seen and not heard

Let teenagers' parties provide practice for adult responsibilities.

- Lay down the ground rules and help with preparations only if asked; let your child plan it his or her way.
- Discuss arrangements beforehand, though.
- At the party, be seen only occasionally and heard only if sought.
- If you feel things may be getting out of hand, talk to your child quietly. Let him or her try to get things back on track, and intervene only when they give up.
- For food, suggest lots of DIYs for guests – sundaes; customized sandwiches and pizzas; baked potatoes with a variety of fillings; waffles with a dozen toppings; build-your-own canapés.

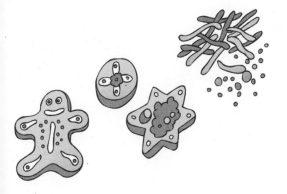

465. Child-sized choices

Children love choices. And changing their mind! Pay attention to your child's input but remember:

- The younger the child, the fewer the guests.
- Let your child make his or her own invites (with some help).
- For younger children, restrict DIY to garnishing – ice cream toppers, biscuit decorations, relishes for burgers or hot dogs, and dips for crisps.
- Plan the activities yourself. For under-10s, set time limits on each game.
- Unlike with teens, constant adult (or responsible teen sibling) supervision is necessary.

467. Remember my party last summer?

For special occasions and children's parties, mementoes are crucial.

- Take lots of photographs! Arm several people with those disposable cameras you can pick up in the supermarket.
- Try to have one of each guest to take home or send a print later with the 'thank you' note.
- Take time over the party bags. Yes, sweets are a treat, but something that'll last longer will keep memories fresher. Attention span depends on age: balloons for three-year-olds, personalized jack o' lanterns for seven-year-olds, potted pansies for 11-year-olds.

■ Please come to my party!

468. Message in a bottle

Invite friends to a cocktail party with a wine bottle!

- You'll need clean glass bottles (smoky green is mysterious!).
- Write your invitation in a large, bold hand.
- Roll it up, writing outwards, and slip it into the bottle.
- Use glass paints to decorate the bottle.

469. A sparkling do

For a special birthday or pre-wedding party invite, let the cake inspire you!

- Match plain cards to the bride's chosen theme (or the birthday person's favourite colour).
- Make a little stencil of a cake – two tiers for a birthday; three for a bridal shower.
- Cut out paper cake 'appliqués' in white, yellow, brown or pink.
- Pipe glitter glue 'icing' along the tops of the cake tiers.
- Now switch to metallic ink and black pens.
- For a birthday, draw the correct number of candles.
- For a wedding, stick the bride and groom in! Add intertwined hearts on top and write their names within them.

470. Sweet cards!

Great invites to an infant's or toddler's birthday bash, and for birth announcements, baby showers and christenings or naming ceremonies!

- Print or pen a simple message on visiting cards – occasion, date, time, and the appropriate name/s underneath.
- Punch a pair of eyelets at the edge and attach a lollipop with ribbon threaded through.
- Co-ordinate a pastel to a baby's gender or make it colourful for the under-fives.
- Make matching place cards and party bags – centre a sweet on the card or label and write the recipient's name around it.

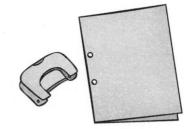

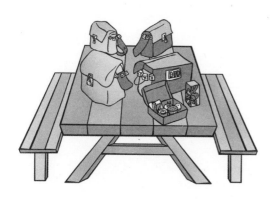

■ Show a fine theme

471. Spelling wizards to tea

Host a 'School Begins!' or back-to-school party for preschoolers and nursery newbies.

Serve a cold assortment meal:

- Pinwheel sandwiches made by cutting wraps in slices
- Cherry tomatoes and baby carrots
- A carton of frozen yogurt or chilled juice
- A bite-sized biscuit, mini muffin or slice of carrot cake. Pack each portion in a lunchbox and pop it into a small satchel.

The fun bit:

- Spell the child's name on the handle with letter beads on string – scrambled!
- Add some maths? 'Seal' each satchel or lunchbox with luggage locks – coded to open on solving a sum!

472. Barbecue Sunday

A barbecue can liven up a family gathering; no need for a separate children's meal either!

- Make the lunch a sit-down, calm affair.
- Pipe each child's name on a plate in ketchup; use mustard for the grown-ups.
- Serve potato smileys with the meal.
- Have fruit sorbets in cones to round off the meal.

473. Skip to my tune

Outdoors means less wreckage indoors, especially with excited young guests around. Little girls should be thrilled with skipping on the lawn.

You'll need:

- A skipping rope each – look for fun handles; send these with the invite or give as early party favours.
- Sugar-free lemonade.
- Music on a portable CD player or radio.
- A stopwatch and timer for long skips.
- Cold spaghetti and meatballs for lunch.
- Fairy cakes for tea: place loops or coils of liquorice or strawberry lace on each to resemble a skipping rope; add bits of jelly worms for handles.

474. Hula-hooping jamboree

Another active outdoor theme – with hula-hoops!

Serve:

- An assortment of pretzels and bread rings with dips for snacks
- Loopy straws for drinks
- Bagels or spaghetti hoops for lunch
- Grilled pineapple and coconut ice cream for afters.

When they get tired, have flowers – real or silk – to hand to make garlands with. Then some slow music for hula dancing!

475. Bead workshop

Just what little fingers need to stay occupied indoors (Warning: not suitable for under-fives).

- Arrange a 6-cup muffin tray or ice tray for each child.
- Fill each cup (or cube) with a variety of beads, charms, string, wool, ribbon and elastic bands, old buttons and dried pasta shapes (wheels, hollow twists, tubes).
- Let them share alphabet beads.
- Put a tray of supplies where everyone can reach it – fabric glue, fabric scissors (for over-12s), clasps.

Each guest takes home the bracelets or necklaces she made; or the children can do a swap.

476. Dip-your-own sleepover

Pyjama parties mean midnight munchies.

- Keep a big bowl of popcorn with the stack of (parent-policed) DVDs.
- Before leaving the kitchen, lay out muffin trays with age-appropriate nibbles.
- Fill the cups with pretzels, mini biscuits, flavoured yogurt, toffee sauce or dulce de leche, shredded coconut, cereal or rice crispies, crushed nuts, jams or preserves.
- Leave one cup empty and cover each tray with clingfilm, adding the guest's name on a sticky note.
- Add an ice cream scoop with a note to your child permitting <u>one</u> ice cream tub! That's for the empty cup…
- Gift each child a funky little torch – practical and pleasing!

477. Pod-swap party

Teens and tweenies can get together with their favourite tunes and knitting needles! Making cases for each other's MP3 players is super-easy — a rectangle that needs doubling up and sewing along the edges!

You'll need:

- The contents of your old workbasket
- Sequins, jewels, felt patches, braid and trimmings
- A pair of knitting needles apiece; a couple of crochet hooks for the seams and lanyards
- No-drip, no-crumbs snacks: baby carrots and slices of peppers; breadsticks, pitta wedges or pretzels (no messy coatings!); pieces of fruit (not too juicy!), chorizo and cheese on cocktail forks or toothpicks; drumsticks with the ends wrapped in foil; meatballs on cocktail sticks; rice paper parcels (well-sealed!) of dried fruit; fortune cookies…
- Drinks in swig bottles or sippers.
- Music

478. Literary larks

How about a reading session for the budding writers?

- Have your child send each guest a pocket-sized journal and a pen (get different colours of ink for each) – the invitation on page one asks the recipient to compose a small piece to share at the soirée.
- Provide letter-shaped biscuits, ginger beer or hot chocolate.
- To warm up nervous speakers, add fortune-and-fun notes (jokes, challenges, compliments) written on rice paper with edible ink. Fold them small and print names on them (or leave in a lucky-dip bowl), or put out a stack of paper and stand the pens in a beer mug.

479. Spa luncheons

These are great for any gang of girls, young or adult!

- Invite: Gel eye masks or a scented candle with the date and time scribbled on with a marker.
- Dress code: Robes, slippers and a towel – guests can change at your place.
- Goodie bags: Transparent plastic or terry towelling (tip: make from old shower curtains or towels!); fill with hand towels, face mask*, nail polish, nail files, scented oils, rose water, shampoo and lotions.
- Supplies: Cotton wool balls and pads; soothing music CDs; scented candles; hair dryer; curlers and irons.
- Menu: Fruit juices and smoothies; crudités, fingers of rye bread and dips; salads; dried fruits and nuts; fresh fruit and dips.

*Note: Unless you know your friends' individual skin types, stick to basic, hypoallergenic gels or peel-offs.

480. Popcorn and a movie

Gone too long without seeing your best pals?

Organize a Saturday night at your home theatre – with the children asleep!

- Serve popcorn in cartons.
- Serve fruit juice or sparkling water in bright plastic tumblers with a twirly straw.

■ Pat-a-perfect-cake

481. Alien celebration

The easiest 'shape cake' must be the spaceship!

- Bake the cake – a sturdy Madeira – in a pudding basin.
- Upend it to serve.
- Cover with ready-roll icing.
- Decorate with sweet shapes in different colours.
- For tentacles and antennae, stick in liquorice, fruit laces or lollipop.
- Sprinkle on some fizzing sugar candy or paint with food glitter for the 'metallic' effect.
- Cover the cakeboard in dark blue icing and cut out stars, moons and a few clouds.
- Or fashion it as a landing site with almond rocks, chocolate-chip gravel and brown-sugar 'sand'.

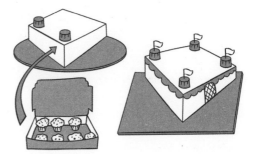

482. Crowning castle

Another super-easy cake is a castle.

- No need to bake specially – buy a square chocolate cake and a box of muffins.
- Cover each cake separately in ready-roll icing (upending the muffins) and assemble the smaller ones on top of the square to make towers.
- Line up mini marshmallows to crenellate the battlements!
- Use a large chocolate wafer for a drawbridge – cut out the entry. Stick on with jam or melted chocolate.
- Add chocolate stick flagpoles and make flags from icing or fruit leather pieces.
- Make the turrets from sliced Swiss rolls.

483. Fairy cakes? No, a princess party!

Another straight-from-the-supermarket idea.

- Get enough fairy cakes, a little frosting or butter cream and some pastel-coloured ready-roll icing. Buy some red or purple sugar (or liquid food colouring) and assorted hundreds-and-thousands or sugar sprinkles.
- Peel off the paper cases, turn over the cakes and cover in frosting.
- Colour the sugar and sprinkle on top.
- Roll out the icing and cut into strips twice as wide as the width of your cakes.
- Using a biscuit cutter or the back of a large piping nozzle, scallop one edge of each strip.
- With dabs of melted chocolate on a cocktail stick and tweezers to pick up the sugar sprinkles, decorate the straight edge of the strips.
- If you have stamps for decorative shapes, use the nozzle to cut out those shapes from the middle of the icing strip.
- Let dry before cutting the strips into lengths to match the circumference of the cakes. Press in place gently. Leave to dry.
- You can paint over the crowns with metallic food colouring.

484. Sweet flowerpot

Make a garden-proud pal a container-garden cake.

- Sterilize a well-fired ceramic flower pot.
- Bake your cake in it.
- Cover the top with heaped brown sugars. Add some instant coffee granules and a couple of nutty white-chocolate rocks.
- Put about a dozen fairy cakes – preferably the pale golden kind – in metallic green cases for 'flowers'.
- Smear some melted chocolate in the centre of each cake. Press in a large flat chocolate button or some chocolate chips to make the flower centres.
- Cut ready-roll icing or sugar paste into petal shapes – triangles, teardrops or hearts.
- With a dab of melted chocolate or some frosting coloured to match, anchor the petals in overlapping circles around the centres.
- When dry, stick each flower on a strand of straight green ribbon pasta and push it into the flowerpot cake.
- Add leaves cut out of green leather or sprinkle some green hundreds and thousands beneath!

485. Balloons for baby

Babies aren't impressed by cake shop offerings.

- Make a bunch of balloons – speckled, sparkly or animal shapes – the birthday centrepiece. Tie each to a short strand of spaghetti and stick in the cake – making sure it won't float away!
- Each little friend could take one away after the party.

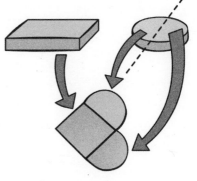

486. With all our hearts

Versatile and easy – to buy or bake – is the heart-shaped cake.

- No cake mould? Bake a cake in a round and a square cake tin – the round should have the same diameter as the side of the square. Halve the former and fit the semicircles against two adjacent squares –a heart!
- For a romantic or feminine feel, cover in pink or peach ready-roll icing. Sprinkle the top and plate with heart or flower-shaped candy. Use sugar paste flowers as candle holders.
- For a grown-up feel, use red icing and chocolate hearts.
- For a younger theme, stripe multi-coloured icing across the top or polka dot with colourful buttons or mini macaroons.
- Or just cover the top with chocolates.
- Whatever the theme, tie a ribbon round the cake – use a dab of royal icing or melted chocolate to anchor it in the crease on top, let dry, then make the bow.

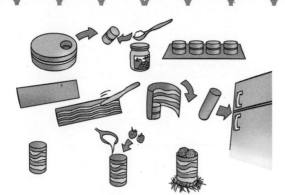

487. Cake chocolate boxes

This is an impressive, individually portioned cake.

- Stamp out 6-cm/2½-inch rounds from a pair of sandwich cakes. Lightly smear some jam along the sides. Line up on a baking sheet or platter.
- Cut strips of baking paper or buttered greaseproof paper into strips 9-cm/3½ inches long and about 2½ times as high as the cake pieces.
- Melt chocolate. Working quickly, use a palette knife to spread it on the strips, completely covering one half lengthways.
- Extend some horizontally into the other half, creating a wavy top edge to the chocolate strip.
- Still working quickly, wrap each strip, as soon as it's done, around one round of cake. Take care not to overlap the paper at the end; let any excess stick out. Chill to set.
- To serve, pipe whipped cream in the hollow and fill up with strawberries. Tie a ribbon around the chocolate case or encircle the base with rosemary.

488. Chocolate wings!

With white or dark melted chocolate, a paper icing cone and a little practice, you can make pretty butterflies flit around.

- Fill a greaseproof paper cone with melted chocolate.
- On a sheet of greased paper or baking paper, pipe the letter 'B'.
- Next to it, pipe a mirror image! (For practice, use a runny paste of flour and water.)
- You can fill in the wings with squiggles.
- Pipe as many pairs of wings as you want.
- Make as many bodies – a small dot joined by a long oval and then a longer leaf shape.
- Leave in the refrigerator for 45 minutes.
- When ready to use, peel off the paper and assemble your dessert plate on a piped cream swirl or a flower squiggled with berry-flavoured ice cream topping in a squeeze bottle. Or prop it directly in a soufflé, sundae, mousse or other creamy pudding.

489. Cupcake sundae

Ridiculously easy but novel for a summer party.

- Have a small muffin or fairy cake for each guest.
- Divide a large quantity of thick yogurt and tint with food colouring – think of ice cream flavours. Chill until firm enough to whip stiff.
- If you like, mix in crushed pralines, nuts, chocolate wafers and chopped fruits into some of the yogurt.
- Thread each muffin on a skewer to allow you to hold it up while you cover it with the chilled yogurt.
- Pile the muffins into a large deep glass dish, preferably a long boat shape, and garnish with wafers, chopped fruit and drizzled toppings.
- Chill until ready to serve, with dollops of sorbet or frozen yogurt.

490. Party chickens

Eggs and chicks are good for a birthday bash too.

- A simple theme for a larger party uses marshmallow chicks. Or you can use candy or sugar-coated almond 'eggs' instead.
- Line up a pie dish of butter cream and a plate of desiccated coconut shreds coloured green.
- Holding a muffin by its case, first dip its 'face' into the butter cream and then the green coconut 'grass'.
- Refrigerate to set while you make chocolate flakes by running a peeler along the thin edge of a chocolate bar.
- Wearing disposable plastic gloves, make 'O'-shaped chocolate nests on top of each cupcake. A basic round will do – the hollow isn't necessary but is nice for adding depth.
- Sit a yellow marshmallow chick on the nest, or add a clutch of three eggs each.

491. Animal craters

For a zoo or circus-themed party, children will love filled pastry shells.

- Use animal-shaped cutters to cut puff pastry. You'll need three of each to make one animal.
- Keep one of each shape whole and cut a circle out of the other two.
- On a baking sheet, stack carefully with the intact shape as base and the cut shapes overlaid.
- Brush with egg and bake till well risen. You will get a case similar to a vol-au-vent.
- Fill the animals' bellies with cooked vegetables or a salad.

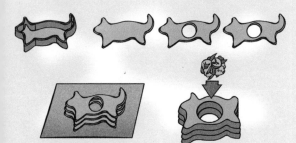

492. Caterpillar-ed cakes!

For a quick kiddie party, get a box of assorted fairy cakes with:

- Liquorice laces or strawberry string
- Some desiccated coconut
- An assortment of small sweets
- A set of round chocolate 'beads'
- Ready icing.

Now
- Make a green lawn for Mr Caterpillar. Colour the coconut with green food colouring and spread in a large plate.
- Place the cupcakes on it in a large curl, leaning them against each other – stick together with extra buttercream if need be.
- Prop the last cupcake sideways on top of the one before it.
- Pipe on his face with icing in a piping bag, or stick on sweets for his features.
- Add liquorice legs to each segment and pop the end into a chocolate bead 'foot'. Give him antennae too.

■ Exciting extras!

493. Stop/Go! sundae

A fun idea for a children's party to go with the automobile cake – traffic light parfait!

- Set jelly in green, yellow (or orange) and red colours. Chop up small.
- In clear tumblers, layer slices of kiwi and green jelly first.
- Follow with orange segments or melon or mango pieces and amber jelly.
- Finish with rosy-skinned apple pieces, cherries or berries in the red jelly.
- Add a whipped cream or custard hat.

494. Fruit split

A healthier traffic light dessert.

- In oval ice-cream dishes, lay a spliced banana as if for a banana split.
- Use fruit scoops shaped with a melon baller.
- Try kiwi for green, cantaloupe melon for amber and watermelon for red.
- Top with toasted sunflower seeds and pomegranate seeds.

495. Bubbly for all!

While the grown-ups pop the cork, give the children their own bubbles.

- Give them a party phial – wide-mouthed mini wine bottles are perfect – filled with soap solution and a bent wire loop each.

Cleaner than confetti!

496. Serve a sweet spoon

A luscious surprise – a chocolate-coated coffee spoon!

- Melt couverture chocolate (or run your fondue fountain) and dip the spoons in to cover – it may take 2–3 dips to get a really rich robe on them.
- Dry them bowl-down on a tray or baking sheet lined with waxed paper.
- Store in a cool place.
- For an extra-special touch, dip the spoons in a bowl of sugar right after the chocolate – choose vanilla-infused, cinnamon-flavoured, golden or mix in some dried lavender.
- Or bake some biscotti swizzle sticks and coat the ends the same way.

In cool weather, use these to decorate party bags. Tie to a bag of sugared almonds or give each guest a boxful.

497. Crackers with your coffee?

Sometimes it would be nice to take a party bag away from a grown-up party!

- For a 'grown-ups only' dinner party, serve your own crackling cantuccini in transparent paper. Tie with red or gold ribbons. Guests can dip them into coffee or port, or take them away.

498. Sweets for the sweet

Fudge is easier to make and as sweet as hand-dipped chocolates.

Use biscuit cutters to punch out:
- Flower shapes for Mother's Day (dot the centres with a chocolate kiss)
- Valentine hearts to lay in pink paper cups
- Stars for Christmas
- Chick shapes for Easter
- Fudge faces
- Plain squares tied up with shoestring liquorice.

499. Boat race

For a tiny tots' pool or tub party.

- Make paper boats from different colours and add ring-shaped sweets along the inside 'decks'.
- Fly a different flag on each, supported by a cocktail stick and tucked into the central peaked fold.
- After the sweets have been munched, launch a boat race!

Warning: Adult supervision is needed throughout.

500. Bacchus' wreath

For a really mythical touch for a spring garden party:

- Drape ivy around the wine bottles and/or the ice bucket!

Notes

Notes

Notes

Index*

*Please note: The numbers shown refer to page numbers rather than tip numbers.